D1237098

The Decade of
Elusive Promise

Studies in
American History and Culture, No. 5

Other Titles in This Series

The Decade of Elusive Promise

Professional Women in the United States, 1920-1930

by Patricia M. Hummer

RESEARCH PRESS

Library of Congress Cataloging in Publication Data

Hummer, Patricia M   1946-
  The decade of elusive promise.

  (Studies in American history and culture ; no. 5)
  Bibliography: p.
  Includes index.
  1. Women in the professions—United States. I. Title.
II. Series.

HD8038.U5H85 1978   331.4'81   78-27674
ISBN 0-8357-0986-8
ISBN 0-8357-0987-6 pbk.

CONTENTS

TABLES

CONTENTS

CHAPTER I

WOMEN WORKERS IN THE 1920's

At the Seneca Falls Convention in 1848, the formal launching of the woman's movement in the United States, the leaders drew up a "Declaration of Sentiments" that enumerated the ways man tyrannized over woman. Among the list of political, legal, and social handicaps was the following grievance:

> He [man] has monopolized nearly all the profitable employments, and from those she is permitted to follow, she receives but scanty remuneration. He closes against her all avenues to wealth and distinction which he considers most honorable to himself. As a teacher of theology, medicine, or law she is not known.[1]

The participants passed a resolution enjoining members to work for "securing to woman an equal participation with men in the various trades, professions, and commerce."[2] Seventy-two years later, women had won the vote, seen many of their legal and social disabilities removed, and increased their numbers in all levels of gainful occupation, but they still had not secured "equal participation in the profitable employments."

Women had entered the world of business and the professions, but not without great struggles. On the threshold of the twenties, career women—those gainfully employed women, most often in business and the professions, who chose their lifework not simply out of economic necessity but because they enjoyed their particular occupations and found them important to their existence—realized they still had many battles ahead of them. Winning the ballot had removed only one more obstacle. Although conditions had improved, women still did not have equal opportunities in advanced training, job placement, advancement, recognition, or pay. An editorial in an early issue of *Independent Woman,* the official magazine of the National Federation of Business and Professional Women's Clubs, commented on the task ahead:

> . . . there is still a battle on, the fight for economic equality. There is no folding of feminine hands in prospect. If men's work is from sun to sun, women's work, as always, is never done.[3]

Despite such realistic appraisals, many career women were hopeful about their economic future. Indeed, they had reason to be. Events prior to and during the early twenties as well as such indicators as the general employment trends of the female labor force and articles in the media suggested a bright future for business and professional women. More young women than ever before were seeking careers and many were combining them with marriage and families, suggesting that they thought such a path was a viable alternative to the traditional female role of homemaker and mother.

Since the 1870 census, the first to tabulate the labor force by sex, the number of gainfully employed women had risen steadily. This trend accelerated after 1900 with the continuing influx of immigrants and the rapid expansion of cities and industries.[4]   Between 1900 and 1910, the number of female workers rose from 5,319,397 to 8,075,772 (51 percent) where the number of males rose from 23,753,836 to 30,091,564 (26 percent).[5] Women increased their representation in the labor force from 18 to 21 percent. Not only did they enter industry and customary female occupations such as teaching and nursing, but also women replaced men almost entirely as clerical and secretarial workers and as telephone operators.   The gradual movement of women into business and the professions quickened as their numbers doubled in those fields.[6] There was no reason to expect this growth to slow down or die in the second decade of the century.   Of course, in 1910 few expected a war.[7]

The United States declared war on the Central Powers on April 6, 1917, and the Armistice was signed on November 11, 1918.   During that short period, American women proved to be capable and efficient workers.   A munitions manufacturer reported favorably:

> We are pleased to state that the enthusiasm, patriotism, and earnest endeavor of the women workers were the mainstay of this plant, and as we received an Ordnance Flag for production, the results are conclusive of the effectiveness of their work.[8]

Women filled all kinds of jobs created by the emergency or stepped into positions vacated by soldiers.[9-]   Those already in the labor force, particularly in domestic service or in marginal jobs in industry, found better-paying jobs in the war factories.[10]   It was the first time that women worked in some heavy industries in more than miniscule numbers.[11] Professional women also made the most of the war period to secure better employment.   As nurses and doctors they voluteered for military service, though in the latter capacity they had small success.   As lawyers, they served as advisors on exemption boards and preparedness committees.[12]

As had been true in other wars, women who stayed at home volunteered their services.   The Federal Government, under pressure from women's groups, created the Committee on Women's Defense Work within the Council of National Defense (CND) to coordinate the volunteer activities of those groups. The Women's Committee, made up of the luminaries of national women's organizations and chaired by the redoubtable feminist, Dr. Anna Howard Shaw, was restricted to an advisory role. Nevertheless, Dr. Shaw nonplussed the gentlemen of the CND by effectively coordinating women's volunteer services through the network clubs at her disposal.[13] Women sold bonds, collected food and money, rolled bandages, and clothed the French, winning praise for their services and spirit.

For many men, war-time experience provided their first close contact with female workers. In some cases, the contact led to a reduction in prejudice against women. Fred W. Morse, chief of an experimental station at Massachusetts Agricultural College, stated that there had been a natural aversion to hiring women until one was actually forced to do so. "I think, however, that prejudice has disappeared from the minds of nearly everybody connected with our laboratories," he added.[14] Female lawyers in New York City also found openings because of the temporary scarcity of males. Having demonstrated their abilities, some of the women became permanent members of the firms where they had worked on a trial basis.[15] A few factories reported finding women "so satisfactory" that they planned to employ "an even greater proportion of them than the present labor scarcity necessitates."[16] Little by little, the performance of women during the crisis helped chip away at the myth of feminine incompetence.

If the war opened a few doors for women, the Armistice signalled an end to the brief interlude. The combination of closing war plants and returning veterans created a serious unemployment problem. Because women were the last to join the labor force, many people thought it only fair that they be the first to leave. "'The same patriotism which induced women to enter industry during the war should induce them to vacate their positions after the war,'" said the leader of the Central Federated Union of New York, voicing the view of a portion of the American public.[17] More than a few women complied with the request.[18]

Since female workers were no longer needed for emergency service, it was not surprising to find some of the old injustices and prejudices reappearing. During the war, for example, Miss C. M. Hoke had been one of a group of women to receive an assistantship from the chemistry department of Columbia University. After the Armistice, despite their competence and the needs of the rapidly expanding university after the war, the women were summarily replaced by men, not all of whom were veterans. Miss Hoke was more fortunate than some of the other women; she managed to complete her degree without the financial support provided by the assistantship.[19] Clearly, women's contributions were welcomed in times when there was a shortage of personnel, but intolerance reasserted itself when that condition ceased to exist. As a consequence, many of the opportunities arising from the war were short-lived.[20]

Most of the benefits that did result from the war were indirect. For some women the experience meant a widening of their perceptions. Many industrial workers in war plants regulated by the government, for example, discovered for the first time what it meant to earn adequate wages and to work in conditions that did not enervate mind and body.[21] Some school teachers realized that occupations other than minding small children were more suited to their talents and interests.[22] New fields, such as personnel work, welcomed talented females, and a number of women found the courage to tackle even the more characteristically male fields.[23] Female workers made psychological gains as their self-respect and confidence grew: they saw themselves as professionals making important contributions rather than stop-gap workers filling time.[24] They had learned something of the value of work.[25]

If the war awakened some women to their abilities and the scope for using them outside the domestic sphere, the suffrage movement intensified that propensity.[26] Furthermore, female participation in the war effort weakened resistance to the Nineteenth Amendment and speeded its passage.[27] The acceptance of women as equals in the electorate indicated the further disintegration of attitudes which had limited their participation as gainful workers. Many Americans predicted the position of women—economic and social as well as political—would alter following their enfranchisement.[28]

Whatever hopes were cherished concerning the magical power of the ballot, its benefits for the economic status of women were primarily indirect. The vote did not automatically grant equality in the marketplace, as business and professional women well knew.[29] And yet the psychological value of having the right to vote was difficult to deny. As a potentially powerful voting bloc, women could no longer be lightly dismissed as unimportant members of society.[30] Then too, possession of the vote gave some women renewed vigor to carry on the quest to remove their remaining legal, social, and economic disabilities.

More concretely, the Nineteenth Amendment helped clarify the ambiguities of women's legal status. In non-suffrage states prior to 1920, female attorneys had been severely handicapped because their status as citizens and legal persons had been suspect, and holding most elected offices had been out of the question.[31] Suffrage helped settle both problems. After enfranchisement, Lucille Pugh, a lawyer with thirteen years of experience in New York City, noticed that she was greeted with "marked cordiality" when she entered the courtroom, a "decided difference" from five years earlier.[32] A different kind of problem arose in a small Michigan town at the end of 1920. One William Leibnitz refused to answer a summons from the justice of the peace, Mrs. Pheobe Patterson, on the grounds that, as a wife, she was chattel and not a person at all. Therefore, she could not hold office. Henry A. Mandell, Judge of the Circuit Court of Detroit, disagreed with Leibnitz's reasoning and ruled that the Nineteenth Amendment had granted the right to hold office as well as vote.[33] Women all over the country hastened to take advantage of their new status. Despite the late date of ratification of the Amendment (Aug. 19, 1920), many women ran for office in November of that year and some were victorious. Over thirty women served in state legislatures in 1921, and by 1922, there were at least fourteen women serving as mayors of small towns across the nation.[34]

Women who had worked for the war effort and who voted clearly deserved more than the second-class treatment that government had customarily bestowed on them. Confronted with the prospect of a female voting bloc, Washington officials tried to compensate for their earlier oversight by re-evaluating their policies concerning women. Implicit in their actions was a recognition that women had other roles besides homemaking and motherhood.

Severe labor shortages during the war made female workers an attractive alternative to reduced production in a time of pressing need.[35] Because some of the jobs were considered dangerous or difficult for women to perform, the National League for Women's Service urged the Federal Government to set up a women's bureau.[36] In July of 1918, the Women in Industry Service (WIS) was organized for the dual purpose of discovering how best to use womanpower in industry and how to safeguard women's health in war plants. The WIS recruited women for new jobs, studied the effects of night work, state laws, and wages on female workers, and set up standards for war industries.[37]

After Armistice Day, the WIS urged the government to recognize the permanent status of working women by establishing definite standards for government-owned plants and by embarking on an educational program to alert the public to the need for protective legislation. The director's pleas fell on receptive ears. Congress first extended the life of the WIS by a year and then, in June of 1920, gave it permanent status as the Women's Bureau of the Department of Labor.[38] The expectation that the Nineteenth Amendment would be ratified in time for the November elections undoubtedly influenced some of the legislators.

The Women's Bureau had power only to investigate and make recommendations, and its inadequate budget limited the scope of its activities. Nevertheless, not only did it become the major source of information on working women, but it also produced a report that caused the government, the largest employer in the nation, to reappraise its own policies toward women workers.[39] The Bureau conducted a survey of women in the Civil Service from January to June in 1919, during which time the Service held examinations for 260 positions. The investigators found that, because of the use of procedures established in 1870, women were excluded from 60 percent of all tests and from 64 percent of the tests for scientific and professional positions. Men were excluded from only 3 percent of the exams.[40] Not surprisingly, 91 percent of all females, as opposed to 48.5 percent of the males, received clerical appointments. The study also revealed that in the rare cases where females made it into the higher, non-clerical fields, they might receive a salary that was from 16 to 50 percent lower than that of a man with the same kind of position.[41]

The report exposed the illogical and discriminatory policies that the Civil Service had used for half a century, and it shocked officials into action. Five days after "Women in Government Service" appeared, the Civil Service Commission ruled that all exams be open to both sexes. The new regulations, however, allowed department chiefs to specify which sex they preferred when making appointments. Senator George P. McLean of Connecticut went one step farther; he introduced a bill to eliminate all discrimination except where a physical barrier would impair the proper performance of duties.[42] Nothing came of the bill, but it illustrated the concern that at least some Americans felt about the problem of discrimination. Following the example of the Federal Government, some state civil services conducted their own surveys and updated their regulations.[43] It would be several years before women could evaluate the full impact of the rulings, but at the time, it marked another step forward.

Government improved in women's esteem not only because of the Civil Service reform but also because of its new policy of appointing a few women to high level positions. The trend actually began as early as 1912 when President Taft made Julia Lathrop, an early resident of Hull House in Chicago, head of the newly organized Children's Bureau. During World War I, women served on several committees connected with defense efforts. Feminist Dr. Anna Howard Shaw and her colleagues coordinated volunteer activities through the Women's Committee of the CND, while Mary Van Kleek, an instructor in labor problems at the New York School of Social Work, had charge of the WIS. Dr. Elizabeth K. Adams, head of the Women's Educational and Industrial Union in Boston, developed a national referral service for trained women as head of the short-lived Women's Collegiate Service.[44] At the same time, women continued to receive appointments that were unrelated to the emergency. President Wilson, an opponent of the suffrage movement when he entered the White House, experimented in 1918 by appointing Katherine Sellers, an attorney, to be Judge of the Juvenile Court of Washington, D. C., and Annette Abbott Adams, another lawyer, to be the first female United States Attorney. Mrs. Adams was promoted to Assistant Attorney General and was eventually replaced by another woman. The appointment of women continued after the administration changed from Democratic to Republican: President Harding, mindful of the feminine support for his campaign, appointed women to judgeships, chairmanships, and heads of bureaus.[45]

Some of the appointments may well have been little more than a form of tokenism. Being head of the Women's Bureau or judge of a juvenile court did not carry the same prestige, power, or salary as being head of the Census Bureau or a circuit judge. Yet the women's positions were highly visible and not merely honorary. By performing their duties competently, the women often won reappointment or were replaced by other women. Their actions illustrated better than feminist rhetoric that women were capable of holding high level positions that carried many responsibilities.

The popular magazines played a part in familiarizing the public with the notion that women could work outside the home in all kinds of occupations. Periodicals of every sort, from the intellectual *New Republic*, to the feminist *Woman Citizen*, or the family magazine *Delineator*, carried articles on the new breed of woman and her activities. Even the *Ladies' Home Journal*, which had opposed woman suffrage, followed the trend.[46] Some writers deplored the increasing tendency of young women to seek gainful employment, alluding vaguely to the "risk to the community," or citing the transformation of "young, pretty girls into good businesswomen," who missed their chances for marriage.[47] Such negative articles, however, were counterbalanced by those presenting a sympathetic picture of the female worker.

Very early in the twenties, certain kinds of articles became almost standard. The female Horatio Alger story usually described how the widow without experience nevertheless made a fortune, or how sheer determination and natural ability enabled a woman, who had never attended college, to climb to the top of the business ladder.[48] Readers apparently enjoyed the "feminine firsts" variety of article which informed them about women in unusual fields or the awards and honors they had won.[49] And for those who wanted more than vicarious experience, periodicals offered reams of advice on choosing occupations and succeeding in them.[50]

Journalists painted an attractive image of feminine achievement in the business world, but one which bore slight resemblance to reality.

At times, they made little distinction between working girls in lower level clerical jobs and career women. Most articles minimized the effort, time, money, and talent required to secure and keep a good position. Writers sidestepped the controversial issue of combining marriage and career by focusing on spinsters and widows forced by circumstances to support themselves or on blithe young girls who would quit their jobs when "Mr. Right" appeared. Despite distortions, omissions, and misinformation, the articles in popular magazines informed the public about the wide variety of occupations women filled and offered alternative roles to those of wife and mother.

No matter what the glossy accounts in magazines implied about the ease with which women were finding fame and fortune, business and professional women knew from their own experience that it was quite otherwise. Scrimping and saving, teaching for a few years to earn enough to pay for special training, attending night school, having the door to a school or business firm shut in their faces because it did not allow females, enduring professional isolation, and trying to convince the public of their capabilities were more characteristic features of the lives of earlier career women. Consequently, they were encouraged by signs that forecast an earlier path for young women just choosing or entering their vocations.

Professional women watched expectantly as the barriers disintegrated. After years of closed doors, the majority of professional schools began admitting women. Although some of the leading institutions, such as Harvard and Columbia, clung tenaciously to their all-male traditions, it was now possible for women to get quality training for professional careers.[51] Women lawyers, who had been prohibited from entering the bar in all but twenty states in 1900, found they could practice in any state but Delaware in 1920.[52] No state prohibited a qualified female physician from hanging out her shingle.

Since professional organizations provided means for keeping abreast of developments in the field, securing positions, and controlling the profession, exclusion from membership was a handicap for women. Trained women had endured this kind of professional isolation for years but finally gained full membership in national associations in the decade prior to the twenties.[53] Women doctors and lawyers, who had struggled for half a century and more to win acceptance from their male colleagues, interpreted these events as a start in the right direction.

At the same time that the professions were relenting toward female practitioners, businessmen appeared to be actively courting feminine approval. Manufacturers and salesmen had already learned from studies on consumer behavior that women were the major spenders of family income, and they were determined to find out what appealed to feminine tastes. Who knew better than another woman what the average housewife would buy?[54] The new field of advertising provided many young women with opportunities while college graduates with degrees in home economics found a demand for their expertise in manufacturing.[55] Banks and investment firms interested in female patronage established women's departments. After Columbia Trust Company in New York City announced in 1919 that it had appointed Virginia Furman Assistant Secretary in charge of its women's department, society women and feminist organizations promptly transferred their accounts to the bank. Within two years, six other major banks in the city had installed females in prominent positions or opened their own women's departments.[56] Almost any business that employed girls or catered to female customers offered scope for the talented and ambitious woman.[57]

Many career women were determined to take advantage of the expanding opportunities and to help their sisters in business and the professions as well. Even the most successful among them could remember how they had been handicapped in their careers by their isolation and scarcity. One reason teaching remained a dominant profession for females was that there was a scarcity of guidance toward other careers and professions.[58] Prior to 1910, the placement offices of Smith College and the other Seven Sister schools had functioned merely as teachers' agencies.[59] Alumnae had difficulty discovering positions other than teaching in their communities. Existing literature on available jobs, their prerequisites, and how to obtain them was scanty at best.

By the early twenties, many colleges had expanded their teachers' agencies into full-scale occupational bureaus, and alumnae groups, the American Association of University Women, and the YWCA, either individually or together, had established local vocational bureaus for women in major cities across the nation. The non-profit organizations were not strictly employment agencies, but they did gather information about local opportunities and maintain listings of trained women seeking employment. Following World War I, several of the directors of the bureaus decided to pool their resources and discover precise information about different occupations.[60] Consequently, they formed the National Committee of Bureaus of Occupations. Each unit made studies of local conditions for career women, but the backbone of the information came from the Bureau of Vocational Information (BVI), an offshoot of the Intercollegiate Bureau of Occupations for Trained Women in New York City. Between 1919 and 1926, the BVI published several excellent studies on individual vocations and a massive volume on the training available to women in the professions and allied occupations..[61]

The vocational bureaus did not work alone in their educational endeavors; other interested groups amplified the work they had initiated.

A growing stream of vocational literature assisted guidance counsellors and young women planning careers.[62]   Business and professional women's clubs took an active part by providing speakers for colleges, high schools, and organizations, and by starting scholarship funds.[63] Even young women still in training formed special sororities and clubs to encourage others of their sex to develop professional goals.[64]

Women's associations did more than just advertise the glories of a career to the younger generation. A number of the organizations had been founded because of the exclusion policies of male associations and because of the helplessness that women felt in combatting massive discrimination alone.[65] Perhaps they learned the value of solidarity and organization from observing the suffragists, but in any event, career women joined together to share their problems and develop solutions for them. The female associations also tried to provide all of the features that characterized their masculine counterparts. Women appear to have thought the organizations were productive because between 1910 and 1920, at least twenty national and countless local associations were founded, and their memberships grew annually.[66]

Feminine solidarity extended beyond the various clubs and into the marketplace as well. One commonly-held belief was that women themselves would not patronize or help their sisters. In the early twenties, however, events appeared to contradict this view. As already noted, women could and did consult female bankers and investors. If they travelled to either New York or Washington, D.C., they could stay in women's hotels managed by members of their sex.[67] A female architect and contractor designed tidy, easy-care dwellings to fit the requirements of busy career women.[68] Because of their sex, business women often had difficulty buying insurance for their companies. Lena Madesin Phillips, one of the growing legion of insurance saleswomen, decided to specialize in this area, not only because it was good business but also because she liked to work with women.[69] Countless professional women trained "daughters" to succeed them, and business women helped young women get started.

The efforts of concerned business and professional women and of guidance counsellors appeared to bear fruit. As a result of programs for vocational information, a decided shift away from teaching became noticeable during the mid-teens and accelerated during the war years.[70] The post-war reaction to female workers had not discouraged younger women from seeking gainful employment.[71] Furthermore, more women than ever before were attending colleges and professional schools: in 1920, they made up 47.3 percent of the total enrollment in institutions of higher education.[72] These signs, in conjuction with recent events, could be interpreted as indications that women were not only increasing their numbers in the labor force but also making determined efforts to improve their status within it.

Until the results of the 1920 census appeared at the end of 1922, it was impossible to gauge either the numerical growth of the female labor force or the extent to which women had moved into the profitable employments. Subjective impressions gained from the media or observations of events in a local neighborhood encouraged many people, including some who closely observed the female work force, to think in terms of a "female invasion" of the labor force. Two economists estimated the number of women in gainful occupations at over 11,000,000, a view shared by Dr. Elizabeth K. Adams, director of both the Boston and federal vocational bureaus.[73] In 1921, the *Woman Citizen* quoted the Women's Bureau's estimation of 15,000,000 working women in an article.[74] It must have surprised these people to learn that there were only 8,549,511 women in gainful employment in 1920, an increase of only 473,739 over the 1910 figure.[75]

The Women's Bureau explained how the mistake in their earlier estimation could have been made:

> When a woman dropped out of domestic service or gave up dressmaking to work in a munition factory or to become a streetcar conductor, the entire community heard of her new employment, but no one mentally subtracted her from the ranks of those in her former occupation. . . .[76]

The Women's Bureau was discouraged to learn that between 1910 and 1920 the proportion of women who worked dropped from 23.4 to 21.1 percent and that females made up a smaller part of the total work force, declining from 21.2 to 20.5 percent between 1910 and 1920.[77] Certainly the over-all statistics were nothing to boast about.

On closer examination of the data, however, researchers discovered that the picture was not quite so bleak as first appearances had led them to believe. When compared with the statistics of male workers, those of the female labor force did not seem too bad. Although the number of gainfully employed men had grown by 2,973,373, the proportion of men over the age of ten in the labor force had declined from 81.3 to 78.2 percent, or 2.4 percentage points more than the proportion of women in the labor force had declined.[78] Furthermore, of the 572 occupations listed, only twenty-nine showed an increase for one sex and a decrease for the other. In all other cases, both sexes rose or fell together: if the number of women in medicine or agriculture fell, so did the number of males.[79] Occasionally, the rate of growth for women was more than a hundred percentage points higher than the male rate, but such occurrences usually resulted from the smaller base number of women.[80]

The statisticians were rather perplexed by the small growth rate of both the male and female portions of the labor force, so they looked for causes. They noticed that two categories of employment had declined dramatically between 1910 and 1920:   there were 982,551 fewer males and 723,373 fewer females in agriculture, and domestic and personal service had lost 23,370 men and 344,297 women.   Census officials thought that some of the reasons for the drastic reduction in agricultural workers might include over-counting in 1910; changing the census date from April 15 in 1910 to January 1 in 1920, or from a busy to a slack season; new instructions to enumerators causing them to ignore seasonally unemployed persons; and the war, which lured many farmworkers into military service or factories.[81] The rural to urban shift of the general population may also have been a contributing factor. Moreover, the war affected domestic service because it almost eliminated immigration, a prime source of servant girls, and because higher pay in war plants attracted other servants.

The decrease of 1,067,670 women in agriculture and domestic service altered the character of the female labor force. A major shift occurred away from blue collar and toward white collar employment. There were 1,421,632 more women in transportation, trade, professional service, and clerical work in 1920 than in 1910, a growth rate of 74.8 percent. In 1910, 76.2 percent of all female workers were engaged in agriculture, domestic service, and industry, and only 23.7 percent were in white collar jobs and the professions; in 1920 the first category had dropped to 60.9 percent and the latter had risen to 39.2 percent.[82] Women made up 47.4 percent of all professional workers, and female librarians, nurses, and ministers had doubled their numbers while women laywers, chemists, and university professors and presidents had tripled theirs.[83]

The kind of women who went to work had changed somewhat during the ten-year period as well. While the number of native white women in the labor force had grown by over a million, the number of foreign-born and black women had dropped by more than half a million, despite increases of all three classes in the general population. Native white women had increased from 59.7 to 68.4 percent of the female labor force.   The reduction of agricultural work hurt black women in particular: in 1910 farm work had supplied 52.2 percent of the 2,013,981 black women with jobs, but after the decline of 438,876 farmworkers, only 39 percent of the black women earned a living that way. Foreign-born women decreased most in domestic service, a total of 161,115, though they showed a surprising decline in industry.[84]

In comparison to black and foreign-born women, native white women, both of native parentage and of foreign or mixed parentage, had prospered over the decade. It was these women who benefited from the expansion of white collar jobs and professional positions.[85] In terms both of numbers and of domination of particular fields, the native white woman of native parentage made the greatest gains. Since it was this group that supplied the majority of the middle class, the increases of native white girls could be interpreted to mean that, on the whole, more middle class women were entering the labor force than ever before. The shifts from blue to white collar occupations further indicated a move toward better jobs and wages.

Insights into the changes in the female labor force were probably lost on average Americans who, after all, obtained most of their information from a local newspaper or magazines and not from perusing the census volumes. Most of the periodicals gave scant attention to women when discussing changes in the population. Even the feminist magazine, *Woman Citizen,* only mentioned the increases in very odd and obscure occupations.[86] Americans were apparently more interested in statistics about the growth of their own communities, the shift from farm to city, the numerical increases of Japanese, and the proportionate decreases of blacks, Indians, and immigrants.[87] The average citizen probably continued to form his opinion of the working girl from indicators immediately available to him and not from statistics in obscure government publications. The revelations from the census did not lessen debates surrounding equal pay, protective legislation, and working wives and mothers, though all sides quoted figures to support their arguments. For the most part, the female worker now appeared to be an accepted part of American society: her numbers had increased, she was slowly improving her occupational status, and she was important enough to merit an entire census monograph devoted to her.[88] Opportunities for advanced training, better paying jobs, and positions in business and the professions were opening all the time. After the initial recession of 1921, the decade became one of the most properous in American history. There was no reason to suspect that women would not share equally in the economic boom.

In fact, the hoped-for economic gains for women did not materialize during the twenties despite their numerical increases in the labor force. Women workers increased their numbers by 25.8 percent with the addition of 2,202,605 new members. While the proportion of adult males in the labor force declined, that of women rose.[89] In 1930, women made up 22 percent of the work force. As in 1920, the census showed the expansion of female employees in white collar jobs and the professions: the addition of 1,346,806 women in trade, clerical positions, and the professions accounted for 56 percent of the feminine increases.[90]

As for the working woman herself, slight changes were again noticeable. The restrictive immigration policies of the twenties augmented the domination of native white women who made up 68.4 percent of the female labor force.[91] Although the largest age group of working women remained between twenty and twenty-four years, a continued reduction of child labor and an increasing number of older women in gainful employment meant that the median age of the female labor force was gradually rising.[92] Significantly, more married women than ever before were gainfully employed. In 1920, only 9 percent of all married women worked outside the home and they made up 23 percent of the female labor force; in 1930, those numbers had risen to 11.7 and 28.9 percent respectively.[93]

Although women were joining the labor force in large numbers, they were not rising significantly within it. Women declined proportionately to men in agriculture and manufacturing and increased in clerical work, but shifts in the male-female ratio of other occupational categories were minimal. The occupational trends begun a decade or two earlier had continued throughout the twenties.[94] The exception was domestic and personal service which reversed the trend of 1920 and grew by nearly a million new members. The category included personnel in a wide variety of restaurants, hotels, and service businesses, all of which grew considerably during the decade. Even so, there were at least 400,000 more women working in private homes as cooks and servants.[95] Women who had to work and had few skills to offer went into this low-paying and exhausting labor: very young girls, older women, widows and divorcees, and black women.[96]

Higher on the occupational ladder, women did not do much better. For most young women "going into business" meant becoming a salesgirl, secretary, or clerical worker. Although some businesses, such as banking and real estate, opened their doors to women, men still outnumbered female employees, and women clustered in subordinate positions.[97] Statistics reaffirmed the belief that most young women wanted a job only until they married because the high participation rate of women between the ages of twenty and twenty-four was followed by a considerably lower rate for women between twenty-five and thirty-nine.[98] Although this pattern was visible in all occupations, it was most marked in clerical work, the haven for the young, middle class woman.

Professional women, on the whole, were more likely to work longer than secretaries, but otherwise the picture for them was equally discouraging. Although this category increased by 509,251, the growth included 46,251 new semi-professionals and attendants. Significantly, school teaching, despite a slight proportional decline, was still the largest female profession. In 1930, three-fourths of all female professionals were either teachers or nurses, while dentists, physicians, lawyers, and college faculty combined constituted only 2.1 percent of the category.[99] Although there were twice as many female lawyers in 1930 as in 1920, their numbers were so minute that they made up only 2 percent of the legal profession. More disturbing were the numerical decreases of women doctors and dentists at a time when the number of males in those professions was rising.[100] Of the learned professions, only in higher education did women make concrete gains: they doubled their representation on faculties and made up 32 percent of the profession in 1930. Even in this field, however, women were concentrated in the lower ranks with heavy teaching loads and poor pay.[101] As in other occupational categories, professional women had not made advances in male fields but had congregated in a few "female" occupations.

Ten years after the Nineteenth Amendment, women knew that they had not produced startling changes in the political and social systems and that they had not carved out an equal place for themselves in the economy. On the contrary, they appeared to have failed to make good use of the widening horizons presented to them at the beginning of the twenties. "Viewing my actual experience I realize how little I have played the role of the new woman my friends and I talked so much about ten years ago," confessed one woman.[102] Many among the younger generation of women obviously wanted to work, but careers were either beyond their aspirations or beyond their reach. The clustering of females in a few occupations and in the lower ranks of most fields suggested that discrimination was still widespread. Indeed, some women experienced bitter frustration at their condition in business and the professions. "The truth is, there is seething dissatisfaction among women from one end of the business world to the other. What distinguishes the exceptionally able woman from her sisters is her resentment," commented an observer.[103] Some career women began wondering if their place were in the home after all as traditionalists and eugenicists had been telling them all along.[104] The optimism of much of the rhetoric of career women in the early 1920's waned as they realized they still had far to go to achieve equal participation in business and the professions.

Career women may have been dispirited by their situation, but not everyone shared their gloomy perception of the twenties. It was widely believed, both at the time and since then, that the decade was an era of economic emancipation for women. Two contemporary observers, journalist Frederick Lewis Allen and historian Preston Slosson, recorded for posterity the astonishing metamorphisis of "the" American woman. Expanding opportunities in the job world took its place among short skirts, bobbed hair, and the new morality as manifestations of the change.[105]   Both authors wrote from the vantage point of the early thirties and relied on keen powers of observation rather than on statistics. As respected members of their professions, they endowed impressionistic images of the new woman with a legitimacy that magazine articles could not, and later historians accepted their impressions as fact.   George Mowry, for example, stated that there were five times as many women in the labor force in 1928 as there had been a decade earlier.[106]   Arthur Link was more cautious in his estimates, but he stressed the relations between women's expanding possibilities of employment and the revolution in manners and morals.[107]   Both authors used the phenomenon of the new woman to illustrate other arguments. Nevertheless, the twenties have gone down in history as a decade of economic emancipation for women.   According to these historians, the hopes expressed by career women in 1920 had been generously fulfilled.

In the wake of reviving feminism in recent years, historians have been reexamining assumptions of earlier generalists concerning the suffrage movement and its aftermath.   Three young historians have produced important works on the post-suffrage era: *Everyone Was Brave: A History of American Feminism* by William L. O'Neill; *The Woman Citizen: Social Feminism in the 1920's,* by J. Stanley Lemons; and *The American Woman: Her Changing Social, Economic, and Political Roles, 1920-1970,* by William H. Chafe.   Despite differences of focus and interpretation, they agree on the question of women's economic emancipation: women did not win economic emancipation or equality during the twenties.

O'Neill links the meager economic gains of women to the failure of feminism.   Because the vote had dominated the woman's movement for years, suffragists had over-estimated its power and neglected to consider problems that would follow enfranchisement.   O'Neill asserts that only by rearranging institutions such as the home and family would women win equal opportunity in the job market.[108]   Unwilling to tamper with these sacred institutions, feminists instead divided over the issue of protective legislation versus equal rights for working women.   The division in the feminist ranks destroyed their political clout and hampered economic advancement because neither program had viable support.[109]   The jaded younger generation lost interest in the squabbles of the older women and pursued personal freedom rather than economic equality.   Feminists had never resolved the career-or-marriage dilemma, and young women were consequently forced to choose between the two. By the end of the decade, growing numbers of women selected traditional roles.[110]

Lemons does not consider feminism in the 1920's a failure, but like O'Neill, he sees a connection between women's economic goals and the weakening woman's movement. Implicit throughout his book is the assumption that the majority of the women in the movement supported the progressive social program of the feminist leaders. Even before suffrage, however, divisions developed along class lines: as career women became professionalized, they narrowed their perspective from broad social issues to limited professional goals.[111] When feminist leaders championed protective legislation for factory girls in the 1920's, career women opposed it because they thought such laws were bad business policy and a threat to their own advance. Working women divided into warring factions which, Lemons contends, not only crippled their efforts for economic improvement but also contributed to the deterioration of the larger woman's movement.[112]

Of the three authors, only Chafe directly examines the economic conditions of women in the twenties. He concludes that inequality was rooted in the social system which divided work according to sex; consequently, most Americans thought homemaking was an appropriate task for women.[113] This preconception affected the employment of women by segregating them into "female occupations" in factories or professions, and curtailed their advancement. Women were ill-equipped to help themselves, and men unwilling to do so. Chafe points out that girls who had been taught how to succeed in the domestic sphere lacked the tools for achievement in the business world. The vast majority of American women accepted the traditional division of labor, thus making more difficult the efforts of a few for economic equality.[114]

O'Neill, Lemons and Chafe have contributed to the comprehension of the post-suffrage woman's movement by unearthing a wealth of information and correcting some erroneous generalizations. They have offered some provocative explanations as to why women failed to improve their economic status in the twenties and have raised questions indicating fruitful avenues for further inquiry. In particular, two analytical problems connected with women's history have appeared which have an important bearing on their interpretations and the future studies of the economic condition of women.

The field of women's history is still so new that it lends itself to broad generalizations. In particular, there is a tendency to consider all women or large groups of women as a totality while neglecting important variations within the whole. Lemons, for example, assumes that all members of the woman's movement—shop girls, career women, or club women—accepted the progressive goals of the social feminist leadership prior to 1920. He then berates those career women who supported the Equal Rights Amendment instead and thus contributed—as he sees it—to the declining effectiveness of the woman's movement. Many business and professional women sympathized with the movement and some participated actively in it. Since most career women held full-time jobs and wished to avoid appearing "radical" in the eyes of male coworkers, it is questionable how much real support they gave even before the question of protective legislation arose.[115] Chafe draws a uniformly dismal picture of the progress of professional women during the twenties, citing statistics of a few groups as evidence. The general reasons for their situation include discrimination, apathy among the younger generation, and socialization. But do these reasons adequately explain why the number of female physicians and dentists declined while women in higher education grew in number and proportion in their profession?[116]

The other major problem arises from women's separateness. Because they form a distinctive group with many problems which are unique to them, it is extremely easy to examine them in isolation and ignore the context. Considering that Chafe, O'Neill, and Lemons discuss the economic condition of women, it is remarkable that they give scant attention to general economic conditions other than the effects of World War I and the Depression. Only O'Neill mentions the high unemployment rate of women from mid-decade onward.[117] The twenties was a prosperous decade, but not uniformly so; certainly agriculture and the textile and clothing industries did not share in the general economic boom.[118] What happened to the workers in these fields, and were other women affected by economic conditions?

Segregating women from the rest of society for analysis can lead to viewing the problems of women workers in terms of their being females rather than in terms of their being workers. Such analysis may ignore the drastic changes occurring in the occupational structure of the economy which affected workers of both sexes. How can one examine professional women without even a cursory glance at the professions? O'Neill comments on the declining number of female physicians and Chafe on the decreasing number of women medical students between 1910 and 1930 to show the impact of low motivation and discrimination. Unlike Lemons, they fail to mention the rising standards in the profession that forced a number of "schools" out of operation and reduced the number of students and doctors as well.[119]

As a result of analyzing women as a separate entity, an inordinate amount of the blame tends to fall on the women themselves for their failure in the labor market. O'Neill reproaches feminist leaders for their failure to change the system which bound females to the home, and Chafe seems to expect women to undo generations of socialization single-handed. Women made up less than half of the population and only a tiny fraction of the power structure. How were they supposed to accomplish such monumental tasks? While it simplifies research and analysis to view women in isolation, such an approach may, in fact, only contribute to the continued segrgation of women from the main body of American history.

Notwithstanding these methodological problems, Chafe, O'Neill, and Lemons have made important contributions to women's history. Their explanations for women's economic failure during the twenties tell part of the story. And yet, neither they nor anyone else has fully explained why career women, given the apparently expanding opportunites at the beginning of the decade, did not improve their position more than they did. Clearly what is necessary is further research dealing with smaller segments of the female professional group, such as the learned professions of medicine, law, and higher education. Certainly the analysis should consider a comparison between men and women within those professions over time, an examination of the structure and changes of the professions, and an evaluation of the influence of external factors upon the occupations.

NOTES

[1]"Declaration of Sentiments and Resolutions, Seneca Falls Convention, 1848," in Aileen S. Kraditor, ed., *Up from the Pedestal: Writings in the History of American Feminism* (Chicago: Quadrangle Books, 1968), 185.

[2]Ibid., 188.

[3]"As Others See Us," *Independent Woman* 1 (August, 1920), 9.

[4]William H. Chafe, *The American Woman: Her Changing Social, Economic and Political Roles, 1920-1970* (New York: Oxford University Press, 1972), 54.

[5]U. S., Department of Commerce, Bureau of the Census, *Fourteenth Census of the United States, 1920: Population, Occupations* (hereafter cited as *1920 Census*), 4:33.

[6]U. S., Department of Commerce, Bureau of the Census, *Thirteenth Census of the United States, 1910: Population, Occupational Statistics* (hereafter cited as *1910 Census*), 4:4.

[7]A. B. Wolfe and H. Olsen, "War-Time Industrial Employment of Women in the United States," *Journal of Political Economy* 27 (October, 1919), 639.

[8]Quoted in U. S., Department of Labor, Women's Bureau, "The New Position of Women in American Industry," *Women's Bureau Bulletin,* No. 12 (1920), 18.

[9]Mrs. Coffin Van Rensselear, "The National League for Woman's Service," *Annals Amer. Acad.* 79 (September, 1918), 275-282; "Are Many Women Replacing Soldiers in Industrial Work?" *Current Opinion* 64 (January, 1918), 60-61; "Women—The Best Munitions Workers," *Illustrated World* 29 (August, 1918), 942.

[10]Wolfe and Olsen, 640.

[11]Ibid.; "New Position of Women in American Industry."

[12]Stanley Lemons, *The Woman Citizen: Social Feminism in the 1920's* (Urbana: University of Illinois Press, 1973), 18-20.

[13]Lemons, 15-17; Nevada Davis Hitchcock, "Mobilization of Women," *Annals Amer. Acad.* 78 (July, 1918), 24-31; William L. O'Neill, *Everyone Was Brave: A History of Feminism in America* (Chicago: Quadrangle Books, 1971), 186-194.

[14]Fred W. .Morse to Beatrice R. Harron, June 23, 1920, Bureau of Vocational Information Papers (hereafter cited as BVI Papers), Box 22, Scientific Work: Chemistry, Arthur and Elizabeth Schlesinger Library on the History of Women in America, Radcliffe College, Cambridge, Massachusetts.

[15]Interview with Miss Lehring, January 30, 1920, BVI Papers, Box 10, Law: Interviews with Women Lawyers; Questionnaire No. 5, n.d., BVI Papers, Box 10, Law: Questionnaires of Women Lawyers in General Practice.

[16] "Are Many Women Replacing Soldiers in Industrial Work?" 61.

[17] "Women's Work after the War," *New Republic* 17 (January 15, 1919), 358.

[18] "Shall Women Lose Their New Jobs?" *Literary Digest* 60 (January 11, 1919), 14.

[19] Quesionnaire No. 30, Feb. 10, 1920, BVI Papers, Box 24, Scientific Work: Chemistry in Metal Work.

[20] Lorine Pruette, *Women and Leisure: A Study of Social Waste* (New York: Dutton and Company, 1924), 60-61; O. Latham Hatcher, *Occupations for Women: Being the Practical Information Obtained by a Study Made for the Southern Woman's Educational Alliance* (Richmond: Southern Woman's Educational Alliance, 1927), xxvi.

[21] "New Position of Women in American Industry," 24-25.

[22] Elizabeth Kemper Adams, *Women Professional Workers: A Study Made for the Women's Educational and Industrial Union* (New York: Macmillan Company, 1921), 18; Wolfe and Olsen, 640.

[23] Marjorie Shuler, "Building Homes For Business Women," *Woman Citizen* 7 (December 30, 1922), 12, 29 (hereafter cited as *WC*).

[24] Adams, 20.

[25] Hitchcock, 31.

[26] "I believe suffrage has broadened the feminine mine (sic) generally, and broken down the prejudice of woman's mind against woman, or women, who are in business and outside-world-work." Questionnaire No. 240, n.d., BVI Papers, Box 10, Law: Questionnaires of Women Lawyers in Business.

[27] Eleanor Flexner, *Century of Struggle: The Woman's Rights Movement in the United States* (New York: Atheneum, 1971), 288-293.

[28] Editorial, *New York Times,* August 19, 1920.

[29] "As Others See Us," 9.

[30] In New York, for example, Republican Senator Wadsworth ran for reelection in 1920. An arch-conservative who had opposed suffrage and every other kind of reform bill, he nevertheless asked women for their votes. He won but received 700,000 fewer votes than Harding did. For more information, see the issues of *WC* between October 2 and November 7, 1920.

[31] Thomas Wood, *A History of Women's Education in the United States,* 2 Vols. (New York: The Science Press, 1929), 2:376.

[32] Interview with Lucille Pugh, April 1, 1920, BVI Papers, Box 10, Law: Interviews with Women Lawyers.

[33]"In Michigan, Women Are People," *WC* 5 (January 8, 1921), 865. Massachusetts made a similar ruling allowing women to run for office. See "Not So Fast," *WC* 6 (July 30, 1921), 20; *WC* 6 (April 22, 1922), 20.

[34]"Pioneers of 1921," *WC* 6 (July 30, 1921), 11; "Her Honor the Mayor," *WC* 6 (March 25, 1922), 10.

[35]"Labor Shortage," *New Republic* 12 (October 20, 1917), 316-217; "Women and the Labor Shortage," *Scientific American* 119 (September 14, 1918), 206.

[36]Van Rensselear, 277.

[37]U. S., Department of Labor, Women's Bureau, *First Annual Report of the Women in Industry Service for the Year Ended June 30, 1919,* 1-20.

[38]U.S., Department of Labor, Women's Bureau, *Second Annual Report of the Women's Bureau for the Year Ended June 30, 1920,* 3.

[39]Ibid., "Women in Government Service," *Women's Bureau Bulletin,* No. 8 (1920), 8.

[40]Whenever a new position was established in the government service, the Civil Service Commission devised a test and qualifications for the applicants, including sex. Once established for one position, those requirements were set for all similar positions throughout the government service. Inertia appears to have been the major problem. Ibid., 10-11.

[41]"Women in Government Service," *Women's Bureau Bulletin,* No. 8 (1920), 24-27; "Women in Government Service," *Monthly Labor Review* 10 (January, 1920), 217.

[42]"Women in Government Service," *Women's Bureau Bulletin,* 7.

[43]Adams, 153.

[44]Martin Gruberg, *Women in American Politics: An Assessment and Sourcebook* (Oshkosh, Wis.: Academia Press, 1968), 116; Adams, 153.

[45]"Woman Succeeds Woman," *WC* 6 (September 10, 1921), 20; "Judge Mary O'Toole," *WC* 6 (August 13, 1921), 20; *WC* 6 (July 2, 1921), 11.

[46]Several of the women's magazines began carrying features on women in activities outside the home after suffrage. See *WC* 7 (September 9, 1922), 27.

[47]"Woman's Place Not in the Bank," *Literary Digest* 64 (March 3, 1920), 143; "Why I Never Hire a Woman under 30," *American Magazine* 90 (August, 1920), 146.

[48]Charles F. Denver, "A Young Woman Who Makes Brooms," *American Magazine* 90 (August, 1920), 75; "Women in $6,000 to $30,000 Jobs," *American Magazine* 88 (July 1919), 60-61, 131-132.

[49]Agnes Lockhart Hughes, "Meet the Lady Bankers, Gentlemen," *Outlook* 127 (March 23, 1921), 462-463; "First of Her Sex in Film Production," *WC* 6 (February 11, 1922), 11.

[50]Kate Douglas Wiggin, "Climbing the Business Ladder," *Outlook* 131 (May 17, 1922), 112-113; "Getting Your First Job and Keeping It," *Woman's Home Companion* 48 (September, 1921), 4.

[51]Out of 129 law schools 102 admitted women in 1920, but neither Harvard nor Columbia did. Beatrice Doerschuk, *Women in the Law: An Anlaysis of Training, Practice and Salaried Positions* (New York: Bureau of Vocational Information, 1920), 25. Harvard also excluded women from its medical school. A number of medical schools admitted women to their first two years of course work but not to the last two years of clinical work on the wards. See BVI, *Training for the Professions and Allied Occupations: Facilities Available to Women in the United States* (New York: Bureau of Vocational Information, 1924), 475.

[52]Doerschuk, 36. Her information conflicts with that of Willystine Goodsell's on which state—Virginia or Delaware—was the last one to admit women to the bar and when the event occurred. See Willystine Goodsell, "Educational Opportunities of American Women—Theoretical and Actual," *Annals Amer. Acad.* 143 (May, 1929), 6.

[53]The American Medical Association admitted women in 1915 and the American Bar Association, in 1918. See Carol Lopate, *Women in Medicine* (Baltimore: Johns Hopkins Press, 1968), 17; Corinne Lathrop Gilb, *Hidden Hierarchies: The Professions and Government* (New York: Harper and Row, 1966), 48.

[54]Beatrice Harding, "The House that Comes to Business," *WC* 6 (August 13, 1921), 11, 16.

[55]Marjorie Shuler, "Of Books and Ads and Stepping Stones," *WC* 6 (November 5, 1921), 11, 17; Bernice Fitz-Gibbon, *Macy's, Gimbel's and Me: How to Earn $90,000 a Year in Retail Advertising* (New York: Simon and Schuster, 1967), 17; Hildegard Kneeland to Beatrice Doerschuk, June 12, 1925, BVI Papers, Box 8, Government and Home Economics: General; Helen G. Atwood to Beatrice Doerschuk, March 30, 1925, BVI Papers, Box 8, Government and Home Economics: General.

[56]"Banking Milestone," *Banker's Monthly* 106 (June, 1923), 1106-1107; Eve Chappette, "Women Workers in Wall Street," *WC* 8 (June, 1923), 13, 24-25; Genevieve N. Gildersleeve, *Women in Banking: A History of the National Association of Bank Women* (Washington, D.C.: Public Affairs Press, 1959), 1-2, 36.

[57]Questionnaires from both women in personnel work and employers in large department stores commented favorably on the improving opportunities for women in both fields in the early twenties. BVI Papers, Boxes 15 and 16, Questionnaires from Personnel Workers, and Box 4, Questionnaires from Employers of Department Stores.

[58]Adams, 399.

[59]"History of Intercollegiate Bureau of Occupations," Women's Educational and Industrial Union Papers, Folder AB, No .5, Arthur and Elizabeth Schlesinger Library on the History of Women, Radcliffe College, Cambridge, Massachusetts.

[60]Adams, 393-399.

[61]See Doerschuk and *Training for the Professions and Allied Occupations.* Two other works published by the BVI were *Statistical Work: A Study of Opportunities for Women* (New York, 1921), and *Women in Chemistry: A Study of Professional Opportunities* (New York, 1922).

[62]Adams, 402-403, 411-414, 424. Adams gives an annotated bibliography of vocational literature available in 1920 on 443-445.

[63]Lemons, 43-48; "New Organizations," *WC* 5 (October 2, 1920), 497; "6,000,000 Business Women," *Independent* 99 (July 26, 1919), 116.

[64]Graduate women in chemistry at the University of Chicago founded Kappa Mu Sigma to encourage other young women. M. Rising to Emma P. Hirth, January 26, 1922, BVI Papers, Box 20, Pharmacy: General. For information on a similar organization for female law students see Frances H. Wilson to Beatrice Doerschuk, n.d., BVI Papers, Box 11, Law: Letters from Women Lawyers.

[65]Zoe Hartman, "Florence King," *WC* 7 (October 7, 1922), 13; Lopate, 17.

[66]Lemons, 58-59. Exact figures for the groups are unavailable. Indications from the National Federation of Business and Professional Women's Clubs, which was a conglomerate of local women's associations, show a steady rise through the twenties. Occasionally, the NFBPWC would publish membership figures. Compare "Carry On," *Independent Woman* 1 (August, 1920), 4, with Marjorie Shuler, "Organization of Business Women," *Review of Reviews* 66 (September, 1922), 309-310.

[67]Winifred L. Rich, "Hostess to Hundreds," *WC* 7 (February 24, 1923), 10; "The New Hotel for Women in Washington," *WC* 7 (December 17, 1921), 14.

[68]Marjorie Shuler, "Building Homes for Business Women," *WC* 7 (December 30, 1922), 12, 22.

[69]Lena Lake Forrest as told to Marjorie Shuler, "I Like to Work with Women," *WC* 7 (February 24, 1923), 10-11.

[70]Adams, 400; Report from Radcliffe Appointments Bureau, 1920-1921, BVI Papers, Box 17, Personnel work in College: Radcliffe; Extract from a report from the Barnard Occupational Bureau, 1924-1925, BVI Papers, Box 16, Personnel Work: Barnard.

[71]Doerschuk, viii.

[72]Mabel Newcomer, *A Century of Higher Education for American Women* (New York: Harper and Brothers, 1959), 46.

[73]Wolfe and Olsen, 639; Adams, 186.

[74]Mary Anderson, "The Women's Bureau, Department of Labor," *WC* 5 (March 5, 1921), 1048.

[75]*1920 Census,* 4:33.

[76]U. S., Department of Labor, Women's Bureau, "The Occupational Progress of Women: An Interpretation of Census Statistics of Women in Gainful Occupations," *Women's Bureau Bulletin,* No. 27 (1922), 2.

[77]Ibid.; *1920 Census,* 4:34.

[78]*1920 Census,* 4:33.

[79]Part of the decline of medical practitioners was caused by reclassifying osteopaths as a group separate from physicians and surgeons in 1920. "Occupational Progress of Women," 29.

[80]"Occupational Progress of Women," 29.

[81]*1920 Census,* 4:20-24, 34.

[82]*1920 Census,* 4: 340, 341.

[83]Ibid., 42.

[84]Ibid., 340, 341.

[85]*1920 Census,* 4:340, 341.

[86]"Where Women Increased," *WC* 7 (February 24, 1923), 22.

[87]"What Ten Years Did to Us," *Literary Digest* 77 (June 23, 1923), 22-23; Malcolm McCaw, "Things Census Takers Learn But Do Not Print," *American Magazine* 97 (February, 1924), 38-39, 108, 110.

[88]U. S. Department of Commerce, Bureau of the Census, *Women in Gainful Employment, 1870 to 1920: A Study of the Trends of Recent Changes in Number, Occupational Distribution, and Family Relationships of Women Reported in the Census as Following a Gainful Employment,* by Joseph A. Hill, Census Monograph No. 9 (Washington, D.C.: Government Printing Office, 1929).

[89]The proportion of men who worked declined from 78.2 to 76.2 percent between 1910 and 1930 while the proportion of women who worked increased from 21.1 to 22 percent; U. S., Department of Commerce, Bureau of the Census, *Fifteenth Census of the United States, 1930: Population, General Report on Occupations* (hereafter cited as *1930 Census)* 5:37.

[90]*1930 Census,* 5:74-75.

[91]Ibid., 74.

[92]Ibid., 115.

[93]Ibid., 272.

[94]*1930 Census,* 5:39.

[95]The exact figures are unavailable because the 1920 census did not distinguish between cooks and servants in private homes and in hotels, restaurants, and institutions. This figure was derived from subtracting the gross figures of women cooks and servants listed in 1920 from the refined figures of 1930 which lists cooks and servants in private homes separately.   Ibid., 48-49.

[96]By examining the tables which break down the female labor force by race, age, and marital condition, it becomes apparent that certain categories of women dominated in domestic service. It was usually the women who were in dire financial straits and had few or no alternative means of support.   Ibid.

[97]Ibid., 46.

[98]*1930 Census,* 5:115-116.

[99]Ibid., 20-21.

[100]Ibid., 48.

[101]*1930 Census,* 5:48; Goodsell, 10-11.

[102]Anonymous, "The Way My Husband Feels About it," *Independent Woman* 11 (September, 1927), 39.

[103]Anne W. Armstrong, "Are Business Women Getting A Square Deal?" *Atlantic Monthly* 140 (July, 1927), 33.

[104]Storm Jameson, "This Independence," *Independent Woman* 13 (October, 1929), 474; Lucy R. Tunis, "I Gave Up My Law Books for a Cook Book," *American Magazine* 104 (July, 1927), 34-35, 172-177; Louis I. Dublin, "The Bachelor Girl—Is She a Menace?" *Independent Woman* 12 (December, 1928), 538, 563-564; Letters to the Editor, *WC* 9 (November 25, 1924), 30 and 10 (June 13, 1925), 30; Anthony M. Ludovici, "Woman's Encroachment on Man's Domain," *Current History* 27 (October, 1927), 21-25.

[105]Frederick Lewis Allen, *Only Yesterday: An Informal History of the Nineteen-Twenties* (New York: Harper and Brothers, 1931), 88-122; Preston Slosson, *The Great Crusade and After, 1914-1929* (New York: Macmillan Company, 1930), 132.

[106]Gainfully employed women rose from 8,549,511 in 1920 to 10,752,116 in 1930. George Mowry, *The Urban Nation: 1920-1960* (New York: Macmillan Company, 1930), 132.

[107]Arthur Link, *The American Epoch: A History of the United States since the 1890's* (New York: Alfred A. Knopf, 1955), 318-321.

[108]O'Neill, vii-ix, 44-48, 264-268, 273-274, 352-358.

[109]Ibid., 230-248, 262-263, 286, 291-293.

[110]Ibid., 302-306.

[111]Lemons, 53, 199.

[112]Lemons, 228-230, 232.

[113]Chafe, viii-ix.

[114]Ibid., 48-111. Chafe summarizes his argument on pages 64-65, 87-88, 109-111.

[115]Lopate points out that medical women tried to blend in with their male colleagues and shunned radical causes which would attract attention to themselves. Lopate, 16-17.

[116]Chafe's figures for women dentists do not match those of the 1930 census which listed 1,287 women dentists, still a reduction from the 1,829 women dentists in 1920. Chafe, 89-92, 93-11; *1930 Census,* 5:47-48.

[117]O'Neill, 247.

[118]Not only had agriculture declined again but the textile and clothing industries, traditional occupations for women, also declined. Independent dressmakers, tailoresses, and milliners dropped considerably in numbers during the twenties. Although some areas of the textile and clothing industries grew, the increases did not offset the losses in other parts of the industry. *1930 Census,* 5: 10, 12, 14, 16.

[119]O'Neill, 304-305; Chafe, 90; Lemons, 42.

CHAPTER II

THE EMERGING PROFESSIONS AND WOMEN PROFESSIONALS

Women in medicine, law, and higher education were hardly representative of the female labor force during the twenties. Altogether they made up less than 1 percent of all gainfully employed women, and compared to the mass of factory and shop girls, professional women enjoyed good working conditions, interesting jobs, and adequate income.[1] Several factors, however, made this group an important indicator of female progress in society. The professions were both male-dominated and high prestige occupations; thus the movement of women into them was significant. Throughout history, achievements in science, law, religion, learning, and the arts—areas dominated in the twentieth century by professionals—have been used as measures of the advance or level of civilization of countries, cultures, and groups.[2] Furthermore, professional women comprised the elite of the female labor force in terms of talent and power. If those in the professions could not improve the condition of their sex, was it reasonable to expect women in blue collar jobs to do so?

To understand fully the ramifications of woman's position within the professions during the twenties, it is essential to know something about the peculiar status of the professions in American society, how each achieved professional stature, and how women first entered this group of occupations. Throughout most of the life of the nation, professions have held a unique position in American society. With no hereditary aristocracy or rigid class system, a person's occupation, either alone or in combination with his education and income, has been the most frequently used measure of social class.[3] Professions stand near the top of the occupational hierarchy in terms of income and prestige. More important, professionals find their work absorbing and satisfying: if they had to start their lives over, most professionals would choose the same careers.[4] Their occupations offer wide range for self-expression as well as a high degree of independence. In general, professionals enjoy a measure of power within their communities, and society accords them respect.[5]

Although many occupations are vital to the smooth running of society, only a few merit the distinction of being professions. Sociologists who have studied occupations have developed an ideal type of profession which has certain characteristics. A profession implies intellectual rather than physical labor, and a person joins this kind of occupation only after prolonged study under the guidance of experts in the theory and application of his specialty. Professionals are expected to have strong motivation for choosing their vocation because they usually make a full-time, life-long committment to it. The work is an end in itself. The kind of work a professional does shapes his relationship with client and community.   His monopoly of specialized knowledge capable of alleviating human problems gives him a certain amount of power and professional autonomy. The tendency to exploit this power is tempered, theoretically, by a code of ethics and objective service. Professionals also have a penchant for forming associations.   The organizations set standards for admission, training, and certification of new members, judge miscreants, and maintain good relations with the public. As the political arm of the profession, the association is ultimately responsible for maintaining its autonomy.[6]

Ideally, a profession should have a full measure of all of the above qualities. At best, some occupations approach the prototype while others actively cultivate certain traits.[7] It is through such a process of professionalization that occupations rise to the status of professions. Medicine, law, and higher learning have traditions extending back to the Middle Ages, but in the United States, they did not really achieve professional stature until the late nineteenth century. At the same time, completely new professions, such as engineering, were beginning to develop. It took certain conditions for professions to emerge. Society had reached a complex stage with many problems and knowledge was expanding rapidly.[8] Significantly, the circustances that made it possible for law, medicine, and college teaching to become professions also increased opportunities for women to leave their traditional sphere and to enter those callings.

The professions in their modern guise did not begin to evolve until after the Civil War, and the process extended over half a century. During that period, the United States changed from a predominantly rural, agruicultural society into an urban, industrial one.   With technological advances and cheap labor supplied by millions of immigrants, manufacturers turned the abundant natural resources into a steady stream of new goods, which improved the standard of living for some classes and enriched the nation. Ready-made clothes, industrial laundries, processed foods gave women more leisure time. The industrial and commercial expansion also enlarged their opportunities for employment. Modern advances were not an unmixed blessing, however. Disease, poverty, and misery ran rampant in congested slums, and the upper classes worried about crime and corruption. The complexity of the problems facing society encouraged the growth of specialized occupations that could deal with them.

Central to the development of modern society, both its problems and their solutions, was the tremendous expansion of knowledge. In the years following the Civil War, the scientific method captured the interest of thinkers who used it to channel random curiosity into orderly question, experiments, and discoveries.[9] Besides adding immeasurably to older disciplines, the knowledge explosion created new fields such as psychology and sociology. A host of scholarly and scientific journals, societies, and research institutes appeared in the United States and Europe that encouraged investigation. Through the marvels of modern science, some men optimistically believed they could solve human and social ills.

At the same time, education was expanding on all levels. States which had not previously done so began public elementary and secondary school systems after the Civil War. Girls benefited as much as boys from the new schools. Only 2 percent of all seventeen-year-olds attended high school in 1870; however, girls, despite their smaller numbers in the general population, already outnumbered boys in the graduating classes.[10] The expansion of public education also provided women with opportunities for employment. Teaching was one of the few acceptable occupations for women, and they gradually took over the field of primary and secondary education after 1875.[11] If female teachers were to prepare boys for college, they would likewise require collegiate training. The female enrollment in normal schools, coeducational institutions, and women's colleges grew from approximately 11,000 in 1870 to 85,000 in 1900.[12]

The appearance of growing numbers of women in classrooms was only one of the many new developments in higher education in the last quarter of the nineteenth century. Indeed, it was high time for change. Since the founding of Harvard College in 1636, the basic concepts of higher education had remained remarkably stationary.[13] Most colleges continued to teach the classical curriculum with its standardized courses. Although the system left little room for individual choice or the introduction of new subjects, supporters of the curriculum pointed its unity and its positive value in instilling mental discipline. The principal methods of instruction—lecture and recitation—complemented the classical curriculum.[14] The college teacher in this system often taught a class all of its subjects. While such a program required a wide acquaintance with the subjects, the very diversity of courses made it unlikely that the tutor would know many of them in depth. Few of the instructors had any special preparation for teaching beyond their bachelor's degree.[15] Many of the tutors were young ministers, themselves recent graduates, awaiting the call to their first pulpit. There were, of course, dedicated and excellent teachers just as there were attempts to reform the curriculum. But the opportunities or incentives for securing advanced training or for changing the curriculum were largely absent in the antebellum period.[16]

The Civil War and industrialization helped to create a climate favorable to experimentation in higher education. Science and technology had shown their usefulness in the war, and the growth of manufacturing encouraged scientific study by creating a demand for trained personnel and by donating handsome gifts for their education.[17] To accommodate the new subjects, colleges gradually adopted the elective system, which provided a greater selection of courses for students and led to the development of specialized teaching and departments.[18] At the same time, the Morrill Act of 1862 established land grant colleges for the purpose of teaching practical subjects, such as agriculture and mechanical arts, which again emphasized the growing trend toward utilitarian education.[19]

The adoption of new courses at both private and state colleges made apparent the scarcity of qualified instructors in these fields. Obtaining advanced, specialized training in the United States was almost impossible before the mid 1870's. Instead, a few Americans studied at the excellent universities in Germany, famous for combining superior instruction and research. The young men returned to the States imbued with novel teaching methods, research techniques, and the desire to start similar universities in America. Johns Hopkins University, the first successful attempt to start a new institution patterned after the German model, opened its doors in 1876.[21] Over the years, the school developed the prototype graduate program which was copied and added to by other institutions.

Other universities followed. Whether they reproduced the Hopkins plan of development or added graduate departments to pre-existing liberal arts colleges, it was an expensive enterprise. The fortunes and gifts of businessmen and entrepreneurs made many of the ventures possible, but the prestige associated with having a graduate school emboldened other institutions to start advanced programs without adequate financial support. By 1900, 150 institutions offered advanced work, though only a third of them had programs leading to the Ph.D. Graduate enrollment grew from 198 in 1871 to 2,382 in 1890 and reached 5,381 in 1900.[22] The number of Ph.D.s awarded increased as well: in 1880, there were fifty-one recipients; in 1890, 147; and in 1900, 359.[23]

Despite the growth of graduate schools, few opportunities existed for women to secure advanced training. Boston University awarded Helen Magill White a doctorate in 1877, but other institutions did not follow the example. Only one female in 1880 and three in 1890 received

Ph.D.s from American universities.[24] Even German universities, which admitted women to classes, did not grant them degrees in 1896. The first dean of Bryn Mawr College, M. Carey Thomas, tried unsuccessfully to pursue her studies at Johns Hopkins and in Germany but finally graduated summa cum laude from the University of Zurich, Switzerland, in 1882.[25] One of Dr. Thomas's goals at Bryn Mawr was the development of a graduate program for women so that others of her sex would not suffer as she had.

The lack of a doctorate was not an insuperable barrier in the academic world for either sex. The number of institutions of higher education increased from 582 to 1,082 between 1870 and 1890, and relatively few of the 15,809 faculty members had a Ph.D. degree.[26] Furthermore, the extraordinary growth of women's education provided many opportunities for female college teachers. Both Matthew Vassar and Henry Durant, founder of Wellesley College, adopted the policy of hiring women faculty members. When Vassar College opened in 1865, it had eight men and twenty-two women on its staff, but seven of the nine top professorships went to men because they had better qualifications.[27] Although most women in higher education taught at women's colleges and normal schools or taught women's subjects at coeducational schools, a few found employment in unusual fields or institutions. Ellen Richards, founder of the home economics movement, taught sanitary chemistry at the Massachusetts Institute of Technology, and Anna B. Comstock, a noted naturalist and illustrator, was the first woman to attain the rank of professor at Cornell University in 1899. Neither woman had a doctorate.[28]

The day when it was possible to reach the summit of the academic world without a Ph.D. was drawing to a close, however. Although graduate work, with its emphasis on specialized research, developed scholars, college officials interpreted the doctorate to mean the holder was well-versed in his field and would be a good teacher. In time, the Ph.D. became primarily an admission ticket to the higher ranks of college teaching.[29] The unrestricted spread of graduate programs, some of which were weak while others were fraudulent, produced doctorates of widely varying quality. In 1900, about a third of all Ph.D.s were awarded for unsupervised work done off-campus or for no work at all; another 8 to 10 percent were honorary degrees.[30]

Men who had spent years earning their doctorates often disapproved of honorary degrees and inferior programs which did nothing to improve either the prestige or the income of the profession. Because of the growing wealth of some institutions and the expense of graduate education, some professors thought they deserved higher salaries than they were currently receiving. Charles F. Thwing warned the profession of the results of low salaries: "The ablest young men are not seeking academic careers. The reasons of this condition are to be found in the industrial, financial, and social relations of American life.[31] College teaching could not compete with business and industry in terms of income.

Efforts to stem the flood of bogus and honorary degrees began in the 1890's. The Federation of Graduate Clubs was founded in 1893 by current and former graduate students who wanted to protect the prestige and economic value of their degrees. They lobbied for higher uniform standards for graduate education and the elimination of honorary degrees, demands echoed by several learned societies.[32] Finally, the agitation culminated in the formation of the Association of American Universities (AAU) in 1900. The largest and most prestigious graduate insitutions were charter members of the AAU, and together they awarded 88 percent of the earned Ph.D.s. The goals of the AAU included: standardization of advanced programs and requirements for admission to them; improvement of weak institutions; and raising the opinion entertained abroad of American doctorates.[33]

Although the member universities complied with the guidelines established by the AAU, only a desire to belong to that association could make non-members conform. It required persuasion from outside organizations to bring weaker programs into line. When steel magnate Andrew Carnegie retired in 1901 and began dispensing his $300,000,000 fortune to worthy causes, he decided to aid higher education by setting up a pension fund for professors of small, indigent colleges. Dr. Henry S. Pritchett, President of M.I.T. and the man Carnegie chose to manage the fund, saw in the Carnegie Foundation for the Advancement of Teaching a marvelous opportunity to "perform all things necessary to encourage, uphold, and dignify the profession of teaching and the cause of higher education."[34] The foundation provided pensions for professors of private, non-sectarian institutions with four-year programs, admitting only applicants with high school diplomas, and having a faculty of at least six full-time professors (interpreted as six Ph.D.s) and an endowment of at least $200,000. Pritchett's plan supported the strongest colleges and forced weaker institutions to bring themselves up to the minimum standards to qualify for membership.[35] The effort to live up to the Carneige Fund standards improved the financial status of the profession and placed a premium on the Ph.D.

Other organizations expanded on the work begun by the Carnegic Foundation in 1906. In 1909, the North Central Association of Colleges and Secondary Schools adopted the first comprehensive set of standards for accrediting colleges. Among the criteria was a requirement that instructors have graduate work equal to that required for a Master's degree and that department heads have doctorates or an equivalent amount of graduate work.[36]   By 1920, other regional accreditation organizations and state legislatures had adopted similar regulations.

The Carnegie Foundation and the accreditation movement had a decided impact on higher education. By defining what constituted a college and setting minimum standards, the organizations not only relegated some schools to a sub-college level but also helped to formalize competition among colleges and universities for students, money, and faculty. The process also encouraged stratification of the academic profession according to what degrees the teachers possessed. Women, as well as men, were affected by this development. Wellesley College discontinued its policy of preferential hiring after 1914 and sought the best available scholars and teachers regardless of sex.[37]

By 1915, the academic profession had gained control over training and, to a certain extent, improved its status and income. But the profession was unusually vulnerable because it lacked autonomy. State universities were at the mercy of capricious legislatures while private institutions had boards of trustees largely composed of businessmen who wanted to run colleges according to commercial ideas. Andrew F. West, a concerned educator, wrote:

> If this is the sum proposition that university education is a business, our faculties are in a bad way, because it means the destruction of their intellectual and moral freedom by reason of the substitution of commercial for academic standards.[38]

The practice of discontinuing courses because they attracted few students alarmed some faculty because they saw it as an infringement on their freedom to teach. Even more distressing was the threat of dismissal if professors espoused, either in class or in public, the "wrong" view on a controversial subject.   In order to protect themselves from such treatment, professors formed the American Association of University Professors (AAUP) in 1915.

In its first *Bulletin*, the AAUP spelled out its views on the relationship between higher education and society: education was the "cornerstone in the structure of society," and science was essential to the development of civilization.[39] If the profession did not have academic freedom, society would suffer:

> Indeed the proper fulfillment of the work of the professorate requires that our universities shall be so free that no fair-minded person shall find any excuse for even a suspicion that the utterances of the university teachers are shaped or restricted by the judgment. . .of inexpert and possibly not wholly disinterested persons outside their ranks. . . .[I]t is highly needful, in the interest of society at large,

that what purport to be the conclusions of men trained for, and dedicated to, the quest for truth, shall in fact be the conclusions of such
men. . .[40]

As the official representative of college teachers, the AAUP filled a gap
in the structure of the profession. It not only tried to protect the rights
of teachers against incursions by college administrators and the public,
but also it established a code of ethics for teachers. The AAUP
continued the discussions begun by the AAU on training and standards
for the profession and on the nature of higher education. The
association did not absorb or supplant the AAU, the Carnegie
Foundation, or accrediting agencies, but by 1920, it was in a position to
cooperate with these organizations to expand on the goals of the
academic profession.

Women participated actively in the founding and running of the
AAUP, indicating their status within the profession. Indeed, the years
before 1920 witnessed a noticeable improvement in the position of
academic women. The number and proportion of female Ph.D.s had
gained steadily: in 1900, twenty-three women and 359 men earned
doctorates whereas in 1920, ninety-three women and 522 men did so.
Because of the growth in female enrollment from 85,000 to 283,000
between 1910 and 1920, women had increased their representation from
18.8 to 30.1 percent in the academic profession.[41] These trends appeared
to be strong in 1920, suggesting that the position of women within
academia was likely in improve.

As in the case of the academic calling, the medical profession
enjoyed a long, if not always distinguished, history in the United States.
Despite attempts to maintain standards of practice at the beginning of
the nineteenth century, by 1870, the medical profession had deteriorated
into a shockingly competitive business.

Many of the problems of the medical profession stemmed from
the low state of medical knowledge. In general, doctors had only a hazy
knowledge of how the body, diseases, and cures worked, and there was
little systematic research before the end of the nineteenth century to
remedy the situation. Ignorance did not prevent physicians from
diagnosing and treating patients, however, and the generally poor health
of the population created a demand for whatever services were available.
Since the treatment often produced adverse results, medical sects and
charlatans using harmless, "natural" therapy made large inroads into the
practices of regular physicians.[42]

The public had little protection from either imcompetent or
unscrupulous doctors. By the Civil War, the few existing licensing laws
and boards had fallen into disuse or had been abrogated by legislatures
that believed in the concept of *caveat emptor*.[43] Self-regulation by the

profession was also nonexistent. All a doctor needed to begin practice was a diploma from a medical school, many of which were strictly business ventures. Because a proprietor's profits came directly from tuition and graduation fees, schools vied with each other for students by shortening courses and lowering entrance and graduation requirements.[44] A doctor could graduate from a medical program consisting of two five-month courses of identical lectures, having passed only five out of nine oral exams, and never having seen a patient or examples of the diseases he was about to begin treating.

Although the state of medical practice was far from desirable, the situation enabled women to enter that occupation in spite of opposition from society and male physicians. Despite the long tradition of midwifery, it was commonly believed that the female was too weak and too sensitive to pursue a medical career. Yet the very modesty which society prized so highly deterred many women from seeking medical advice and treatment from male physicians. Women doctors could serve an important function by caring for those of their sex and for children.[45] Elizabeth Blackwell forged the path for women when she graduated from Geneva Medical College in 1849. Although most regular medical schools remained closed to women, sectarian and marginal schools that had difficulty attracting students welcomed female applicants. Furthermore, the low cost of starting a medical college made possible the founding of nineteen women's medical schools between 1850 and 1895.[46] After 1870, the restrictions on admission eased a bit because women could study at the University of Zurich and because many of the regular medical schools followed the example of the University of Michigan by admitting women to their classes.[47] The elite institutions of the East did not open their doors to women until after 1890, however, and some did not do so until much later.

A diploma from any medical school, no matter how bad, permitted the female doctor to practice. She needed no license, no clinical training, no hospital affiliation, and no membership in a professional association. The woman physician discovered, nevertheless, that it was difficult to start practice because most hospitals would not let her use their facilities and because male physicians often ignored her when making referrals. Most medical societies, including the American Medical Association (AMA), did not admit women, contributing further to their professional isolation.[48] The social stigma attached to female doctors limited their practice to the poor, to immigrants, and to other women. While they appear to have been an uncommonly dedicated group, few women doctors became rich from the practice of medicine.[49] Despite all the drawbacks, women continued to enter the profession: their numbers rose from about 500 in 1870 to 7,387 in 1900.

While women struggled to join the medical profession, the first serious efforts to upgrade the occupation had begun. Spurred on by the example of German universities, where 15,000 Americans studied medicine between 1875 and 1914, a few schools experimented with new curricula, higher entrance requirements, or longer programs. Because such innovations usually caused a sharp decrease in enrollment for a few years, most schools did not follow this pattern. An Association of American Medical Schools, founded prematurely in 1876, died from lack of support and was reestablished in 1889. In two reports in 1883 and 1889, the Illinois Board of Health made the first attempt to rate all medical colleges, including diploma mills. At the same time, licensing boards were reappearing, and in 1891 they formed the National Conference of State Medical Examining and Licensing Boards. At their first meeting, the members discussed the possibility of pressuring inferior schools by establishing high educational standards for admission to the exams.[50]

The logical champion of medical reform was the AMA, which had been founded in 1846 for the purpose of improving medical education. Through the years, the leaders had continued to urge reform. Indeed, Dr. N. B. Davis' inaugural address in 1883 contained all the elements of professionalization: better education, licensing laws, and organization of practitioners.[51] But the rhetoric was never followed by action. Because the AMA had an exclusive membership policy, it had little influence on the average practitioner.

The main drawbacks to reform, however, were the power of the medical schools and the indifference of practitioners. The profit motive was strong among American doctors in the late nineteenth century. Proprietary schools grew like toadstools: the seventy-five schools in 1870 rose to 116 in 1890 and peaked at 166 in 1904.[52] Suggestions to lengthen courses, to add expensive laboratories, or to require high school diplomas for admission met rebuff. School proprietors complained that the cost involved would close many institutions, thus depriving the "poor boy" of a chance to better himself. Standardization, they charged, was an undemocratic attempt to stifle medical freedom and would result in the profession becoming an upper-class occupation.[53] The majority of practitioners, having received the inadequate training under criticism, had reason to feel insulted. Rising standards might also mean reexamination or loss of clients to younger, better-trained practitioners. Doctors were, consequently, not particularly interested in reforming their vocation.[54]

By the turn of the century, however, internal and external forces caused many practitioners to change their minds on the need for reform. The general health of the nation had improved, not because of physicians' skills, but because of better public sanitation, hygiene, and diet. The discovery of diptheria anti-toxin in 1895 revitalized interest in medicine as a science, and philanthropists began financing medical research in schools that agreed to improve their programs.[55]   The progressive reform movement, with its exposés on everything from oil trusts to patent medicines, may have influenced the profession as well. In 1906, the *Journal of the American Medical Association (JAMA)* announced that it would no longer carry advertisements of patent cures.[56]

Perhaps the atmosphere of reform made the profession overly sensitive, but it was clear that a growing number of doctors believed they were losing social and economic status. They measured declining respect of the public in terms of the swelling number of malpractice suits and the expanding proportion of non-medical personnel in health fields.[57] Many physicians realized that the poor services offered by the profession were to blame:

> We have cheapened the medical profession by making it too common and lowering its standards, if not actually as compared with past, at least relatively as compared with scientific advances of the day.[58]

Doctors blamed what they considered to be their poor economic status on the overcrowded conditions of the profession.[59]   A *JAMA* editorial in 1901 stated that there was one physician for every 600 persons in the country, which was more than adequate.   Taking into consideration population growth and other factors, 3,300 new doctors a year would satisfactorily fill the needs of the nation, but the 160 schools produced 6,000 new physicians every year.[60]   More often than not, the blame for both the overcrowded condition of the profession and its low prestige fell on the proprietary and sectarian schools.   The following quote was typical of the articles in *JAMA* which called for reform:

> Our profession should purge itself of the dishonorable and criminal in its ranks as the legal profession disbars its criminal members. It is a duty it owes to itself as well as to the people.[61]

After 1900, the leaders of the AMA and elite medical faculties began to develop the mechanism that would bring about the desired changes. The AMA reorganized itself into an inclusive association and mounted a successful membership drive on the slogan "Organize or die." Between 1900 and 1910, membership grew from 8,400 to 70,000 or 60 percent of all practitioners.[62] The association also increased its political influence with state legislatures and licensing boards.[63]   Four years after reorganization, the 166 medical schools had a record high enrollment of 28,142 students and 5,747 graduates.[64]   It was time to attack the problem of too many poorly trained practitioners. The AMA established a Council on Medical Education which worked closely with the Association of American Medical Schools. After designing a rating scale the Council began visiting schools with the intention of forcing the unfit ones to close. When proprietary institutions accused the inspectors of bias, the AMA commissioned the Carnegie Foundation to conduct a study of the medical schools in the United States and Canada and make recommendations to the profession. For this task, Pritchett chose a noted educator, Abraham Flexner.

When *Medical Education in the United States and Canada*, known as the Flexner Report, appeared in 1910, it shocked both the profession and the American public. After visiting 155 colleges in both countries, Flexner pronounced only thirty as fit to teach medicine and even they, he said, needed changes. An absence of adequate laboratories, libraries, and museums, too little clinical instruction, part-time faculty, ill-qualified students, and insufficient financial support plagued even the better medical colleges.[65] Flexner saved his most scathing indictment, however, for the diploma mills and sectarian schools. Vigorously objecting to their continued existence on the specious grounds that they offered the only route for the "poor boy" to acquire a medical degree, he pointed out that many proprietary schools actually had higher tuition charges than some of the best schools; therefore, low entrance requirements flourished "for the benefit of the poor school, not the poor boy."[66] Such institutions were a waste of human and social resources and were a menace to society, to gullible students, and to the profession.

Flexner agreed with the AMA that there were too many doctors, so he set about applying the Carnegie Foundation formula, strengthening the good institutions and eliminating the worst. He proposed increasing the requirement for admission to medical school to a minimum of two years of college work, a prerequisite demanded at that time by only sixteen schools, to give students adequate preparation.[67] Furthermore, he invited medical colleges to lengthen their courses, add more laboratory and clinical work, and improve their physical plants. Flexner urged institutions to hire full-time faculty members who would receive regular salaries instead of tuition fees as payment. The tremendous expense involved in renovating medical education would close down proprietary schools. Indeed, Flexner thought thirty-one university medical schools situated in cities across the nation would meet all the country's requirement for medical practitioners. To safeguard people against charlatans and incompetents, Flexner recommended upgrading the licensing legislation so that only students from approved schools could take the exams.[68]

The Flexner Report speeded the process of reform in the medical profession. Within a year, the number of schools dropped to 120 with a total enrollment of 19,786.[69]   Most of the surviving institutions immediately began to renovate their programs to meet the stringent requirements set by the Council on Medical Education. In 1914, the 109 medical colleges were rated as follows: twenty-nine institutions received A+; thirty-eight received A; twenty-two, B; and twenty-four, C.[70]   By 1920, among the eighty-eight schools, seventy received A ratings, eight received B ratings, and ten received C ratings. Licensing boards and legislatures cooperated in the effort, and within ten years after the Flexner Report, thirty-three states required two years of college and seven required one year before entering medical school.[71] In the same period, the total enrollment of medical schools fell to 13,798, and graduates numbered 3,047. The number of physicians decreased from 151,132 in 1910 to 144,977 in 1920, giving a ratio of one doctor to every 729 persons.[72]   Health care had definitely improved. Not only were doctors better trained, but the AMA also began rating hospitals and financing much needed medical research.   Within one decade, the medical profession had completely changed its image and won international respect.[73]

Women physicians played no part in making the decision to reform the profession though they were profoundly affected by it. Over the years, they had slowly carved out a place for themselves in medicine. In spite of continued prejudice on the part of the public and attempts of male doctors to limit them to the allegedly uncomplicated, female fields of pediatrics and obstetrics, women went into and succeeded in most branches of medicine.[74] Studies of graduates of 1881 and 1900 from the Women's Medical College of Pennsylvania, the first women's medical school, showed that they compared favorably with male practitioners in terms of earnings and practice. Nor did the women in the studies find marriage an insurmountable handicap to their work.[75] Women like Alice Hamilton, pioneer in industrial medicine, and Florence Sabin, researcher at Johns Hopkins and the Rockefeller Institute, were making valuable contributions to medical science. Opportunities for medical education had increased dramatically for women: in 1904, some 946 women studied at ninety-seven coeducational medical colleges, and 183 students studied at the three remaining women's medical schools. However, some of the best medical colleges, such as Harvard and Columbia, still did not admit women.[76]

By the time of the Flexner Report, the total number of schools had declined to 155, the number of coeducational schools had fallen to ninety-one, and the number of women students was 752. Even though the number of male students had decreased during the same time, Flexner interpreted the female decline as a loss of interest on their part:

> Their enrollment should have augmented, if there is any strong demand for women or any strong ungratified desire on the part of women to enter the profession. One of the other of these conditions is lacking—perhaps both.[77]

Flexner was sure that ample opportunities existed for women who wanted to become doctors, and in the interest of economy, he recommended closing the three women's colleges. In return, he urged coeducational schools and hospitals to be generous in their treatment of women.[78]

The Women's Medical College of Pennsylvania did not follow Flexner's advice but the two weaker women's medical schools did. It was not clear that women received equal treatment from coeducational institutions. Although the proportion of coeducational schools increased by 1920, the number and proportion of women students decreased. Female students and graduates reached a low in 1915 when only 592 women were enrolled in and only ninety-two women graduated from medical schools.[79] Some of the coeducational programs were so new that they did not attract many female students. As the number of places in medical schools decreased, competition for them intensified, and men were more likely than women to win them. As in the case of other minority groups, women may have found that the increasing requirements had placed medical education beyond their means.[80] Just at the time when a medical degree began costing more in terms of time, money, and sacrifices, alternative careers in health care, such as nursing, were expanding. Many women who wanted to care for the sick undoubtedly chose the easier path offered by support positions in health care.[81]

When the medical profession set out to reform itself in 1910, it had been motivated by a combination of altruism and self-interest. The efficient mechanism developed by the reformers succeeded in raising the standards of medical education and health care while reducing unwanted competition. It had not been the goal of the profession to eliminate or even reduce the representation of women in the occupation. In reality, however, the higher standards and longer educational period represented more of an obstacle to women than to men. By 1920, the number of male and female practitioners had declined, but the rate of decline was greater for women than for men.[82]

While medicine and higher education were professionalizing, law went through a similar process. The legal calling had some peculiar problems which slowed its development. By the same token, the law placed certain special restrictions upon women that hampered their entry into the profession.

Like the other two professions, the legal calling was in a chaotic state in 1870. Nonexistent or lax state regulations governing admission to the bar reflected the prevailing opinion that any man had a natural right to practice law. Because of the low entrance requirements and the predominance of apprenticeship training, the thirty-one law schools in the United States offered only weak programs. Twelve had one-year programs, and the rest offered programs ranging between eighteen months and two years. Even Harvard, which had enjoyed a respectable reputation in the 1830's and 1840's, had no requirements for admission or graduation other than a bare minimum of class attendance. To make matters worse, lawyers and judges had contributed to the rampant corruption on all levels of government, bringing dishonor to the profession. No society, individual, or organization exercised control or leadership.[83]

The prevailing low standards of the legal profession did not ease the way for women as similar circumstances had in medicine. One of the few requirements for admission to the bar in most states was that the applicant be a man or a citizen. Women obviously did not fit the first category, and it was questionable if they fit the second. Under common law, women had the distinction of being perpetual minors or non-persons. When she married, a female lost all separate identity from her husband: she could not sue or be sued, sign a contract, make a will, or own property. Such restrictions would prevent a married woman from fully serving her client. As for spinsters, "A single woman is liable at any time to marry," reasoned one judge who ruled against female attorneys.[84] In addition, there were social reasons for prohibiting the admission of women to the bar. Lawyers feared that trials would destroy feminine delicacy because, "it is not the saints of the world who chiefly give employment to our profession."[85] If women were allowed to practice law, the male members of the bar feared it would only be a matter of time before they ran for public office or voted.[86] Consequently, it was 1869 before an Iowa woman, Arabella Mansfield, became the first woman admitted to the bar, and in 1900, only thirty-four states had removed the restrictions against women.[87]

Although few women managed to surmount the obstacles barring their way to the legal profession before the turn of the century, a good many nevertheless studied law. At first, women read law privately in the office of some male relative, but after 1870, a small number of schools accepted female students. The reasons for women's interest in jurisprudence varied widely; some wanted to share in their husband's occupation while others wanted to understand and change the laws affecting themselves and society. Women sometimes studied law for self-protection. Since a recurrent stereotype in history pictured lawyers as unscrupulous rascals particularly in respect to their dealings with helpless widows, it was understandable that some women felt a need for first-hand knowledge of the law.[88]

Not all lawyers, of course, were incompetent or dishonest, and in the 1870's some of the better attorneys united in an effort to improve their profession. Beginning with a group in New York City in 1870, local and state bar associations were founded all over the nation. The movement led to the founding of the American Bar Association (ABA) in 1878. All of the societies wanted to augment the dignity of the profession, and they usually devised codes of ethics and educational standards for this purpose. The ABA established a committee on Legal Education and Admission to the Bar. In spite of their activity, however, the associations made little progress toward their goals. The selective nature of both local and national organizations limited membership to an unrepresentative elite: in 1900, there were 114,460 lawyers in the United States, but only 1,540 belonged to the ABA.[89] The associations lacked grassroots support and, more important, had little influence with the legislatures or licensing boards, which controlled admission to the bar.

The actual impetus for improvement of the profession came from the law schools. The evolution from rural to urban society increased the need for attorneys and made the law even more complex. Young men discovered law schools provided the best training for the new jurisprudence and the best recommendations for future employment. By 1890, there were sixty-one schools, and by 1910, 124.[90] Harvard Law School, under the leadership of Dean Christopher Columbus Langdell, initiated many of the educational reforms that were adopted by the best schools. Among others, he required students to pass three annual exams after 1878, and he raised the admission requirement to a bachelor's degree in 1896.[91] Contrary to dire predictions, Harvard did not die from loss of enrollment but became the trend-setter in legal education.

As an elite group of law schools emerged during the 1890's, communication between them and the bar associations began to disintegrate. A growing number of law professors had no practical experience, which made them ineligible for membership in most bar associations. Practitioners and professors seemed to have disagreed over the future training of attorneys. Some law teachers thought standardization of legal training in approved schools would produce better lawyers and better justice.[92]

The ABA Section of Legal Education, a semi-autonomous body formed in 1893, agreed with the professors, and in 1897, it recommended a high school diploma as a prerequisite for legal training and the extension of the law school course to three years. The suggestion met opposition from inferior law schools and practitioners, the vast majority of whom had learned their trade in law offices and therefore tended to view the professors as ivory-tower idealists.[93] In 1890, only five states had any regulations concerning preliminary general education for prospective lawyers, and the recommendations of the Section on Legal Education created no movement to change the status quo.[94]

With little encouragement from the ABA, the elite schools founded the Association of American Law Schools (AALS) in 1900. The AALS had high membership requirements: a three-year program by 1905; a high school diploma as a prerequisite for admission; and access to or ownership of state and federal law reports. The association gradually increased its requirements over the years by raising the minimum educational prerequisite to two years of college work and specifying the courses to be taught. While the AALS wanted other schools to adopt these standards, it did not join forces with either the agencies that set regulations for admission to the bar or with the Section on Legal Education. The progress in raising educational standards in law moved slowly as a result.

While the AALS tried to improve legal education, part-time and night schools grew markedly in number and enrollment. In 1890, there had been ten part-time schools with an enrollment of 537 students, but by 1916, there were sixty-four such institutions with 10,734 students, which almost equalled the seventy-six regular day schools with their 11,469 students.[95] The schools, many of which were proprietary ventures, flourished because the legal profession was a ticket to political and business careers and to higher social status. Part-time schools provided an efficient way to become an attorney while still earning a living. Members of the lower classes, first generation Americans, and immigrants found this kind of law school fit their needs. Women also benefited from part-time schools which accepted female students more readily than some of the regular day schools did.[96] Although the legal education furnished by part-time schools was undoubtedly inferior to that of such superior institutions as Harvard or Yale, the lesser schools did provide opportunities to individuals who otherwise could not have earned law degrees.

The rapid multiplication of part-time schools after 1900 caused some concern among lawyers, but they had other worries as well. Recurrent complaints about the administration of justice, laws, and attorneys haunted them, Lawyer Richard Olney remarked on the deteriorating reputation of his profession:

> The calling of the lawyer of the present day is scarcely held in the honor that belongs to it, and in the popular mind stands discredited by false and unworthy ideas of its true character.[97]

In an era of reform, the courts and the legal profession were frequently accused of being ultra-conservative.[98]   The mercenary motives of some members of the legal fraternity added to the disgrace of the profession. Growing numbers of lawyers agreed with Robert J. Aley who said that too many attorneys had "neither the ability, the character, or the training needed for the practice of the law. The presence of such men cause severe judgment to be passed upon all members of the profession."[99]

The situation called for action, and many practitioners clamored for greater organization of the profession, higher requirements for admission to the bar, and better legal training. Opposition was not dead, however.   While some practitioners had serious complaints about the inadequacies of modern training, the bulk of the criticism reflected the antagonism of older lawyers against innovations.[100]   One of the die-hards, Harrison Hitchler, declared that most questions of law needed "neither great learning nor exceptional training," pointing out that Abraham Lincoln and John Marshall had managed quite well for themselves and their country without fancy education.[101]   Standardization of training, he declared, would "shut out from us the sons of farmers and mechanics," and tend to "introduce a caste system of the worst sort."[102] Critics feared that higher educational requirements would place justice beyond the means of many Americans because lawyers would pass on the increased cost of their training to their clients.   Not surprisingly, educational reform made slow progress.

Assistance in the struggle to professionalize came from an unexpected quarter—the medical profession.   Both the ABA and the AALS were impressed by the Flexner Report and its results.[103]   By 1916, the quality of medical education, practitioners, and health care had already risen markedly.   In contrast, the legal profession appeared to be declining.   Because of the rapid increase of proprietary schools, the proportion of law students with college degrees and the proportion of students at high quality law schools had declined. Dr. Walter W. Cook, President of the AALS, made a special trip to the ABA Convention in 1917 to tell the Section of Legal Education of these findings and urged greater cooperation between the two organizations.[104] In Cook's view, the need for reform was imperative:

> With the prevailing low standards for admission to the bar, is it surprising that the legal profession is full of incompetents, poorly trained men, who mismanage their clients' affairs and clog the courts with useless litigation?[105]

By the time America entered World War I, practitioners were ready to listen. They relaxed their objections to raising standards when they realized that a "democratic" profession would include Rabinowitz and Civiletti along with Smith and Jones. Immigration had peaked in the years between 1905 and the First World War, and Americans of older stock became increasingly xenophobic. Many lawyers succumbed to this fear as well, and they equated part-time schools with the upsurge of "foreigners" who were entering the profession.[106] Reforming the legal profession by instituting higher standards would eliminate proprietary schools and, with them, what some lawyers considered to be an undesirable element.

With increasing support from practitioners, the ABA hastened to professionalize. By 1920, 12,000 lawyers, or 10 percent of all practitioners, belonged to the national association. To reach other attorneys, the ABA instituted a policy of cooperation with state and local bar associations in 1918.[107] The AALS and the Section on Legal Education began a cooperative effort to devise criteria for rating law schools while the Carnegie Foundation undertook a study on legal education, which would appear in 1921. However, no jurisdiction in 1920 required attendance at a law school or a law degree for admission to the bar, which indicated the open nature of the profession and the size of the task ahead of the reformers.[108]

As far as women lawyers were concerned, it was fortunate for them that the men delayed their efforts to professionalize as long as they did. In the years between 1900 and 1920, one barrier after another had given way. It had become considerably easier for women to secure legal training thanks to the growth of part-time schools. Although a few top schools, such as Harvard and Columbia, still refused to admit women students, other elite schools had slowly changed their policies. There were even two schools for females: the Portia School of Law, a combination day and night school in Boston, and the Washington College of Law in the District of Columbia. The number of women law students grew from 205 in 1909 to 609 in 1915 and reached 1,171 in 1920. In comparison, the male enrollment for 1901 was 19,365; for 1915, 20,997; and for 1920, 19,821.[109]   By 1920, all of the states except Delaware had dropped their restrictions against women lawyers. Women attorneys could belong to at least thirty-four state and sixty-one local bar societies as well as the national association.[110]

Although the institutional barriers had substantially declined, women lawyers still found it difficult to establish a practice.   Male prejudices had not disappeared. "Very few men lawyers exhibit any enthusiasm at the idea of women in the profession," remarked Marion Cottle.[111] She found that women who had studied law in the office of a male relative often practiced in that same office, but those who took law school courses had to prove their worth and determination: "It undoubtedly requires the courage of one's convictions to enter upon a field where opposition is so strong."[112]   Though they complained that men expected "stars of the first magnitude," without realizing the handicaps women had recently overcome, female attorneys were also aware that too many of their sisters had very poor training, a factor whch might account for at least some of the cold reception they received.[113] The 1920 census counted 1,738 women lawyers, but one study estimated that only half of them were in active practice.[114]

In spite of the frustration involved in trying to go into practice, women lawyers were optimistic about the future in 1920. Over the years, they had watched their numbers increase as legal and social barriers diminished. The legal fields appeared to be expanding for women. With the ratification of the Nineteenth Amendment, the new voters began to use their ballot to encourage legislatures to enact or rewrite laws affecting women and children.   Female attorneys participated actively in these endeavors.[115] The greater involvement of their sex in all areas of public affairs and business naturally meant there were more opportunities for women with legal training as well.   As yet, the movement to professionalize the legal occupation had had little impact on women lawyers.

In the wake of social and intellectual developments after 1870, the occupations of medicine, law, and higher learning had begun to professionalize. Practitioners were motivated both by altruistic desire to improve their service to the public and by a self-interested need to safeguard the prestige and economic status of their occupations. To this end, they formed associations, improved their training, established high standards for practice, and tried to obtain more stringent requirements for admission to the profession. All three occupations went through a similar process, but they developed at different rates and achieved different degrees of success by 1920. Success was dependent on a unified plan of action. In the medical profession, the AMA developed a strong grassroots organization and then coordinated its efforts with the state licensing boards and medical schools. By 1920, physicians were well on their way toward achieving their goals of better medical care and greater professional security. In contrast, college teachers upgraded their training and teaching but delayed development of their professional organization until after 1915. They were still groping towards their goals. The legal calling remained divided into two warring camps until late in the teens. Consequently, lawyers had just devised their plan for professionalization but had not put it into action by 1920.

The process of professionalization was bound to affect women in the occupations of medicine, law, and higher learning, even though they had no input in the decision-making process. In each case, women had entered the occupation at a time when standards and requirement were extremely low. The main quality that pioneer women in the fields needed was courage to withstand social and professional ostracism. Over the years, institutional barriers gradually fell, making it easier for females to acquire the necessary training. When the occupations began to insist on higher requirements, women often found that the increased costs in time, money, and dedication had put the calling beyond their reach. In the decade before 1920, the medical profession raised its standards drastically, and the number of women students and practitioners declined. In higher education and law, the fields were still fluid and expanding, and consequently the number of women in them continued to grow. At least two of the occupations had plans for continued improvements on the twenties, which did not augur all to the good for women in those fields.

NOTES

[1] In 1920, out of 8,549,511 gainfully employed women, 19,032 were doctors, lawyers, and college teachers and presidents. In 1930, out of 10,752,116 working women, 30,341 followed those professions. *1930 Census*, 5:47.

[2] Talcott Parsons, "Professions and Social Structure," *Social Forces* 17 (May, 1939), 457; Everett C. Hughes, "Professions in Society," *Canadian Journal of Economics* 26 (February, 1960), 56-57.

[3] Ronald M. Pavalko, *Sociology of Occupations and Professions* (Itasca, Ill.: F. E. Peacock, 1971), 7.

[4] Robert K. Merton, *Some Thoughts on the Professions in American Society* (Providence: Brown University Studies, 1960), 6; Ernest Greenwood, "Elements of Professionalization," in Howard M. Volmer and Donald L. Mills, eds., *Professionalization* (Englewood Cliffs, N.J.: Prentice-Hall, 1960), 17.

[5] Bernard Barber, "Some Problems in the Sociology of Professions," *Daedalus* 92 (Fall, 1963), 673.

[6] Pavalko, 18-19; Edgar H. Schein, *Professional Education: Some New Directions* (New York: McGraw-Hill, 1972), 8; Morris L. Cogan, "Toward a Definition of Profession," *Harvard Educational Review* 23 (1953), 49.

[7] Barber, 671.

[8] Schein, 34; Wilber Ellis Moore, *The Professions: Roles and Rules* (New York: Russell Sage Foundation, 1970), 24, 54-57.

[9] Frederick Rudolph, *The American College and University: A History* (New York: Alfred A. Knopf, 1962), 246-247.

[10] Richard Hofstadter and C. Dewitt Hardy, *The Development and Scope of Higher Education in the United States* (New York: Columbia University Press, 1952), 31; Mabel Newcomer, *A Century of Higher Education for American Women* (New York: Harper and Brothers, 1959), 35.

[11] In 1870, there were 122,986 women and 77,529 men teachers; by 1890, there were 238,397 females and 125,525 males, in 1900, there were 296,474 females and 126,588 males. U.S., Department of Commerce, Bureau of the Census, *Historical Statistics of the United States, Colonial Times to 1957* (Washington, D.C.: Government Printing Office, 1960), 208.

[12] Newcomer, 14-16, 46.

[13] Ernest Earnest, *Academic Procession: An Informal History of the American College, 1636-1953* (Indianapolis: Bobbs-Merrill, 1953), 21-22.

[14]John S. Brubacher and Willis Rudy, *Higher Education in Transition: A History of American Colleges and Universities, 1636-1968* revised and enlarged, (New York: Harper and Row, 1968), 85.

[15]Ibid., 215; Richard J. Storr, *The Beginnings of Graduate Education in America* (Chicago: University of Chicago Press, 1953), 3.

[16]Rudolph, 110-135.

[17]Rudolph, 243-247; Hofstadter and Hardy, 31; Laurence R. Veysey, *The Emergence of the American University* (Chicago: Uniiversity of Chicago Press, 1965), 1-7.

[18]Brubacher and Rudy, 109-113; Earnest, 139-140.

[19]William H. Cowley, "College and University Teaching, 1858-1958," *Educational Record* 39 (October, 1958), 313; Rudolph, 247-252.

[20]Brubacher and Rudy, 117.

[21]Bernard Berelson, *Graduate Education in the United States* (New York: McGraw-Hill, 1960), 6; Storr, passim.

[22]Berelson, 14; U.S., Department of the Interior, Bureau of Education, *Biennial Survey of Education, 1916-1918* (Washington, D. C.: Government Printing Office, 1921), 680.

[23]*Historical Statistics*, 211-212.

[24]Ibid.

[25]Edward T. James, Janet Wilson James, and Paul S. Boyer, *Notable American Women, 1607-1950: A Biographical Dictionary* 3 Vols. (Cambridge: Belknap Press, 1971), 3:446-449, 2:247-249.

[26]Newcomer, 37; Jessie Bernard, *Academic Women* (University Park, Pa.: Pennsylvania State University Press, 1964), 40; *Historical Statistics*, 211-212.

[27]Earnst, 181-182.

[28]James, James, and Boyer, 3:143-146, 1:367-368.

[29]Brubacher and Rudy, 216; Berelson, 12.

[30]Berelson, 24.

[31]Charles Franklin Thwing, *A History of Higher Education in America* (New York: D. Appleton and Company, 1906), 420.

[32]Berelson, 17.

[33] *Proceedings of the Association of American Universities* 1 (1900), 15 (hereafter cited as *AAU Proceedings*).

[34] Theron F. Schlabach, *Pensions for Professors* (Madison: State Historical Society of Wisconsin, 1963), 28.

[35] Ibid., 29.

[36] Berelson, 21; George F. Zook and M. E. Haggerty, *The Evaluation of Higher Institutions, Vol. I. Principles of Accrediting Higher Institutions* (Chicago: University of Chicago Press, 1936), 26-33.

[37] Bernard, 43.

[38] Andrew F. West, "Changing Conception of the 'Faculty' in American Universities," *AAU Proceedings* 7 (1906), 67.

[39] "General Report of the Committee on Academic Freedom and Academic Tenure," *Bulletin of the American Association of University Professors* (hereafter cited as *AAUP Bulletin*) 1 (December, 1916), 24.

[40] "Report of the Committee on Academic Freedom," 25.

[41] *1930 Census*, 5:47; *Historical Statistics*, 211-212.

[42] William G. Rothstein, *American Physicians in the Nineteenth Century: From Sect to Science* (Baltimore: Johns Hopkins University Press, 1972), 44-62.

[43] Richard Harrison Shryock, *Medical Licensing in America, 1650-1965* (Baltimore: Johns Hopkins University Press, 1968), 28-29, 35-37; Rothstein, 108.

[44] Rothstein, 94-97.

[45] Because there was an oversupply of physicians in the second half of the nineteenth century, male doctors may have feared competition from women in gynecology and obstetrics. Richard H. Shryock, "Women in American Medicine," in *Medicine in America: Historical Essays* (Baltimore: Johns Hopkins University Press, 1966), 187; Joseph F. Kett, *The Formation of the American Medical Profession: The Role of Institutions, 1780-1860* (New Haven, Conn.: Yale University Press, 1968), 118-122.

[46] Lopate, *Women in Medicine*, 15; Shryock, "Women in American Medicine," 182, 193.

[47] Shryock, *Medical Licensing*, 51.

[48] Lopate, 17.

[49] Shryock, "Women in American Medicine," 187.

[50] Idem, *Medical Licensing*, 45-47, 53-54.

[51]Shryock, *Medical Licensing*, 47.

[52]"Medical Education in the United States," *Journal of the American Medical Association* 57 (August 19, 1911), 655 (hereafter cited as *JAMA*).

[53]Abraham Flexner, *Medical Education in the United States and Canada: A Report to the Carnegie Foundation on the Advancement of Teaching* (New York: Carnegie Foundation for the Advancement of Teaching, 1910), 173 (hereafter cited as the Flexner Report); Shryock, *Medical Licensing*, 59-60.

[54]David Karl Rosner and Gerald E. Markowitz, "Doctors in Crisis: A Study of the Use of Medical Educational Reform to Establish Modern Professional Elitism in Medicine," *American Quarterly* 25 (March, 1973), 95.

[55]Ibid., 92.

[56]Shryock, *Medical Licensing*, 70-71.

[57]J. C. Bierwith, "The Medical Profession: The Necessity and Benefits from its More Complete Organization," *JAMA* 35 (August 11, 1900), 336; Rosner and Markowitz, 88-89.

[58]"An Overcrowded Profession—The Cause and the Remedy," *JAMA* 37 (September 21, 1901), 776.

[59]"Commercialism in Medicine," *JAMA* 38 (April 5, 1902), 879-880.

[60]"Oversupply of Medical Graduates," *JAMA* 37 (July 27, 1901), 270.

[61]"The Organization of the Medical Profession," *JAMA* 38 (February 1, 1902), 324.

[62]Rosner and Markowitz, 87; "Medical Organization," *JAMA* 37 (July 6, 1901), 30-31.

[63]Bierwirth, 336; Rosner and Markowitz, 87.

[64]"Medical Education in the United States," 654-655.

[65]Flexner Report, x-xi, 36, 44, 82, 137-140.

[66]Ibid., 43.

[67]Flexner Report, 28.

[68]Ibid., 120, 133, 170-173.

[69]"Medical Education in the United States," 655.

[70]"The Classification of Medical Schools," in Carnegie Foundation for the Advancement of Teaching, *Ninth Annual Report* (1914), 67.

[71]U. S., Department of the Interior, Bureau of Education, *Opportunities for the Study of Medicine in the United States*, by George Frederick Zook (Washington, D.C.: Government Printing Office, 1920), 1.

[72]Esther Lucille Brown, *Physicians and Medical Care* (New York: Russell Sage Foundation, 1937), 110.

[73]Shryock, *Medical Licensing*, 65.

[74]Richard C. Cabot, "Women in Medical Education," *JAMA* 65 (September 11, 1915), 947-948; "Medical Education for Women," *JAMA* 38 (May 17, 1902), 306-307; "Medical Education for Women," *JAMA* 38 (May 31, 1902), 1451.

[75]Shryock, "Women in American Medicine," 193-194.

[76]Flexner Report, 179.

[77]Flexner Report, 179.

[78]Ibid.

[79]Lopate, 193.

[80]Rosner and Markowitz, 97.

[81]Shryock, "Women in American Medicine," 195.

[82]Ibid.

[83]Erwin N. Griswold, *Law and Lawyers in the United States: The Common Law under Stress* (Cambridge: Harvard University Press, 1964), 20, 45-48.

[84]"Women as Lawyers: Mrs. Goodell's Case," *Central Law Journal* 3 (March 24, 1876), 186.

[85]Ibid.

[86]Thomas Woody, *A History of Women's Education in the United States* 2 Vols. (New York: The Science Press, 1929), 2:376.

[87]James, James, and Boyer, 2:429-430; Isabella Mary Pettus, "Legal Education of Women," *Albany Law Journal* 61 (May 26, 1900), 330.

[88]Nina Wright Winston to Emma P. Hirth, n.d., BVI Papers, Box 11, Law: Lettters from Women Lawyers; Questionnaire No. 248, BVI Papers, Box 10, Law: Questionnaires from Women Lawyers in Education.

[89]Alfred Zantzinger Reed, *Training for the Public Profession of the Law: Historical Development and Principal Contemporary Problems of Legal Education in the United States with Some Accounts of Conditions in England and Canada* (New York: D. B. Updike, 1921), 206-216.

[90]Robert Stevens, "Two Cheers for 1870: The American Law School," *Perspectives in American History* 5 (1971), 429.

[91]Griswold, 51.

[92]Jerold S. Auerbach, "Enmity and Amity: Law Teachers and Practitioners, 1900-1922," *Perspectives in American History* 5 (1971), 551-557.

[93]Auerbach, "Enmity and Amity: Law Teachers and Practitioners, 1900-1922," *Perspectives in American History* 5 (1971), 565.

[94]In 1920, only fourteen states had any requirements about preliminary education or admission to the bar. Charles E. Clark and William O. Douglas, "Law and Legal Institutions," in Presidents Councils on Social Trends, *Recent Social Trends in the United States* (New York: McGraw-Hill, 1933), 1454-1485.

[95]Stevens, 429.

[96]Woody, 2:373-376; Doerschuk, *Women in the Law*, 27.

[97]Richard Olney, "To Uphold the Honor of the Profession of the Law," *Yale Law Journal* 19 (March, 1910), 342.

[98]Henry M. Bates, "Should Applicants for Admission to the Bar Be Required to Take a Law School Course?" *Case and Comment* 21 (May, 1916), 961.

[99]Robert J. Aley, "Education for the Law," *Law Students' Helper* 20 (February, 1912), 49.

[100]Hampton L. Carson, "An Existing Defect in the American System of Legal Education," *American Law Review* 48 (November-December, 1914), 872.

[101]Harrison Hitchler, "College Graduation as an Entrance Requirement to Law School," *Law Notes* 18 (January, 1915), 192.

[102]Ibid.

[103]Albert J. Harno, *Legal Education in the United States* (San Francisco: Bancroft Whitney Company, 1953), 96; Paul L. Martin, "Should the Standard Law Course Be Extended to Four Years?" *Illinois Law Review* 11 (December, 1916), 335.

[104]Walter W. Cook, "Improvement of Legal Education and Standards for Admission to the Bar," *American Law School Review* 4 (1917), 338-345 (hereafter cited as *ALSR*).

[105]Ibid., 340.

[106]Auerbach, 572-580.

[107]Reed, 216.

[108]Carnegie Foundation for the Advancement of Teaching, *Seventeenth Annual Report* (1922), 86.

[109]Woody, 2:376; Doerschuk, 24.

[110]Doerschuk, 36, 131-133.

[111]Marion Weston Cottle, "The Prejudice Against Women Lawyers: How Can it Be Overcome?" *Case and Comment* 21 (October, 1914), 372.

[112]Ibid.; Doerschuk, 27.

[113]Isabel Giles, "The Twentieth Century Portia," *Case and Comment* 21 (October, 1914), 354; Doerschuk, 29.

[114]Doreschuk, 36-37, 103.

[115]Jean H. Norris, "The Women Lawyers' Association," *Case and Comment* 21 (October, 1914), 364-366.

CHAPTER III

WOMEN AND PROFESSIONAL TRAINING

By the 1920's, the usual procedure for entering medicine, law, or college teaching involved at least some specialized training at a professional school. In sharp contrast to the conditions of a decade earlier, most professional institutions in these fields accepted qualified female applicants. Women had also increased their representation in professional schools: they made up 5.9 percent of the medical students, 36.9 percent of the graduate students, and 5.6 percent of the law students in the United States in 1920.[1] These signs seemed to indicate expanding opportunities for professional women in the future. At the same time, however, the professions were attempting to change their educational programs and standards, ostensibly to produce better practitioners and better service for the public. Although the conditions and results varied from field to field, one fact became apparent as the decade wore on: the policies adopted by the professions affected the number of women who applied for professional training and their chances for acceptance.

Because of the woman's movement and the growing number of female students, one would expect male professionals to have unburdened their souls on the subject of the feminine invasion. Yet the relative absence of articles or comments on women in the professional journals suggests that other concerns were more pressing. The woman's movement, after all, was but one of many changes in the social, economic, and political life of the United States which affected the professions. Society was demanding more and better service of doctors, lawyers, and educators. Although hospitals and public health services had multiplied in recent years, individuals complained about the maldistribution of physicians and the mounting cost of medical care.[2] The expansion of business and urban areas provided lawyers with an increasing number of civil and criminal cases while inventions such as cars and radios created a need for new social legislation.[3] With the return of veterans from Europe after the war, the U.S. Bureau of Education reported that college enrollment had grown by 42 percent between 1918 and 1920.[4] Leaders within each field were not oblivious to demands that would require their own growth and adaptation.

At the same time, leaders of the learned professions realized that they had to balance the wants of society against the internal needs of their associations and societies. Members of all three professions perceived themselves as either losing or having lost status in the post-war era. Like many Americans, they grumbled about the effects of inflation in the early twenties, but their insecurity went deeper. A representative of the legal fraternity, T. J. O'Donnell, analyzed the problem: "It frequently happens, in these days, that 'mere tradesmen' have university educations—something formerly reserved for the nobility, the gentry, and those destined for the learned professions."[5] What would be the distinction of the learned professions when everyone became learned?

To make matters worse, the frequent intrusions of nonprofessionals into the vocational domain of professionals heightened their sense of insecurity. Doctors guarded against the encroachment of charlatans and quasi-medical personnel, such as osteopaths and chiropractors, on the one hand and against governments on the other.[6] Lawyers took a jaundiced view of the hordes of the newest Americans who seemed to be crowding the profession and were dismayed to see banks writing wills and realtors drawing up contracts.[7] Professors complained of being treated like hired help by boards of trustees, administrators, and state governments.[8] Members of the learned professions, when thus threatened, took steps to safeguard the demand for their particular services to society.

Self-interest was not the sole motivating force for professionals; some were concerned with improving the services they provided for the public. Discussions of how to attract the best young men into each field vied with debates on how to train them effectively so that they would meet the future needs of their communities.[9] Because of both altruistic and selfish interests, the leaders of each of the learned professions paid particular attention to the selection, training, and admission of future practitioners. They formulated and adopted policies in the twenties that profoundly affected the number of applications received from both sexes.

The medical profession, with ten years of experience behind it, served as a model for lawyers and academicians. The doctors had developed an effective tool in the form of the American Medical Association and its Council on Medical Education and Hosptials. The Council determined the criteria for admission to medical school, shaped curricula, and influenced which schools would live or die with its accreditation system. Its program had led to improved training and, consequently, better practitioners, as well as a less frequently mentioned restriction of output.

The policies of the Council were not, of course, universally admired. A combination of curricular reforms after 1910 and the interruption created by World War I had sharply reduced the number of medical students to a low enrollment of 12,930 in 1919, causing a decline in the number of practitioners as well.[10] Young doctors flocked to urban areas where there were hospitals and laboratories which they had been trained to use. As a result, not only were doctors scarce in rural areas but also the cost of medical care rose as physicians made use of newer techniques and equipment. The question was whether or not the increased costs were disproportionate as suggested by Dr. Charles F. Painter, a critic of current practices:

> Whoever, therefore, is responsible for introducing into practice the cost-raising features which lead to the diversion of patients to quacks and cultists, without contributing a commensurate practical advantage to the sufferer . . . can be credited with being the cause for the present situation in the practice of medicine. . . . The evidence lays this at the doors of the medical schools and those regulative bodies to whose advice the school authorities have listened.[11]

Demands came from within and without the medical profession for a shorter, less costly training.[12]

The Council on Medical Education denied that a shorter course would produce good doctors or guarantee their living in rural areas. If physicians concentrated in cities, so did the general population; and improved roads, telephones, and automobiles made it unnecessary for a doctor to reside in every hamlet.[13] Although the leaders of the AMA recognized that society could use more practitioners, they opted for quality rather than quantity. Consequently, the Council pursued its program of attempting to better or eliminate the eight Class B and ten Class C institutions while generally trying to improve the quality of the students and their training at acceptable schools.

The Class B and C institutions, which produced 12 percent of all medical graduates in 1920, continued to exist because of lenient rules for licensure in ten jurisdictions. Although thirty-three states complied with the educational standards set by the AMA, seven required only one year of college preparation, six demanded only a high school diploma, and four had no educational prerequisites. One state did not require attendance at a medical school and another state had no licensing exam. In several states, the existence of separate licensing boards for sectarians, a term embracing osteopaths, homeopaths, and eclectics, provided convenient loopholes for the poorly trained.[14] As long as some jurisdictions did not alter their licensing laws, the inadequate schools would persist in turning out poorly trained physicians.

Since the Council possessed no legal power to close the schools, it relied on publicity and accreditation to urge the institutions to improve or to cajole the authorities to take appropriate action. Four Class B schools eventually achieved A ratings and a fifth one merged with a stronger Class A school. In contrast, only one Class C school—Temple

University—raised itself to Class A status after 1920.[15] The remaining Class C institutions made no attempt to upgrade their programs and refused to cooperate with the Council by submitting annual statistics or by allowing inspections. The Council retaliated by warning prospective students away from the inferior schools.[16] In 1923, two of these schools were exposed for selling medical diplomas. As a result, not only did the schools lose their charters in 1926 and 1927, but also thereafter states began to take a closer look at their licensing laws. By the end of 1927, forty-nine jurisdictions refused to examine candidates from Class C schools although two of the boards actually did not have the right to deny admission to the state exam.[17] With this kind of backing, the Council announced in 1928 that it would no longer recognize the remaining Class C institutions whose diplomas were rejected by forty-six states and Alaska.[18] By the beginning of the thirties, therefore, the Council had achieved its goal of eliminating all inferior schools: the seventy-six medical schools in the United States had A ratings.

At the same time the AMA waged war on substandard schools, it also sought ways of improving acceptable programs. In particular, educators concerned themselves with how best to accommodate their programs to the mushrooming field of medical knowledge. School officials observed that the more undergraduate preparation a student had, the more likely he would do well in and complete his medical program.[19] Some schools, therefore, raised the number of college credits they demanded for admission.[20] To furnish students with the best possible training, Johns Hopkins had decided in 1912 to limit the size of its classes instead of admitting anyone who met its stringent requirements. The number of medical colleges following this policy rose to sixteen in 1920 and fifty-four by 1924.[21] The policy gave school officials the option of selecting the best students rather than accepting all those who met the minimum requirements.

Another trend gaining momentum during the twenties was the expansion of training beyond graduation from medical school. As new didactic and laboratory courses crowded the curriculum, clinical instruction began to suffer. To correct this fault, ten states and ten schools required a year of internship for licensure or graduation in the early twenties. By the end of the decade, eleven schools and fourteen states had this requirement and medical leaders recommended it for all graduates.[22] The Council on Medical Education and Hospitals approved 593 general, state, and specialty hospitals with 3,420 internships in 1920, more than enough for the 3,047 graduates. In 1930, 644 approved hospitals offered 5,437 internships to 4,565 graduates.[23] Theoretically, there were enough internships for the women graduates in both years, provided that all of the hospitals that said they accepted women interns actually did so and provided that the women doctors wanted to take their training in the hospitals open to them. Beyond the intern year, some doctors chose to specialize in particular fields of medicine. This required additional training in approved programs and delayed even longer the young physician's establishment of his own practice.

The policies the Council followed during the twenties were extensions of those begun a decade before, but the results were not the same. Despite the reduction of medical schools and higher admission standards, the enrollment grew annually, from 13,798 in 1920 to 21,597 in 1930. Apparently, applicants had adjusted to the stringent specifications set by the AMA. No statistics appeared on the number of matriculants with bachelor's degrees before 1930, but they did appear for graduates of medical schools. In 1910, 15.3 percent of the medical graduates had baccalaureate degrees; in 1920, 43.5 percent had degrees; and in 1930, 70 percent had degrees.[24]

Although the entire enrollment showed a steady increase over the decade, the growth rates for male and female students were unequal. Female enrollment increased to a high of 1,030 in 1923 and then fluctuated in the 900's till it hit 955 in 1930. The rate of growth for female enrollment over the entire decade was only 16.7 percent. In contrast, the number of male students rose from 12,980 in 1920 to 20,642 in 1930, a growth rate of 59 percent.[25] The early upsurge in the number of women students followed by a later one for men students could be attributed to the impact of World War I and the return of the veterans to colleges and professional schools. This was clearly an incomplete explanation, because the number of women attending college grew dramatically after 1920 as well.

An important consideration for prospective medical students of both sexes was cost. The fact that so many students acquired both baccalaureate and medical degrees was a testament either to their own perseverance or to the wealth of their families. Medicine was the most expensive of the professions to enter. While tuition and fees could be relatively inexpensive if the student attended a state university for both undergraduate and medical training, they could be especially costly if the student attended one of the private institutions in the east. Compare, for example, the relative annual tuitions at the University of Oklahoma, one of the least expensive schools, with Johns Hopkins University, one of the most expensive:[26]

1920	Undergraduate Tuition	Medical School Tuition
University of Oklahoma	free	$40-$60
Johns Hopkins	$200	$267
1928		
University of Oklahoma	$50	$113
Johns Hopkins	$400	$410
1930		
University of Oklahoma	$50	$200
Johns Hopkins	$400	$610

Tuition and fees had doubled in a decade on all levels of higher education, and this did not include room, board, books, or incidentals. In 1928, the minimum annual expenses for undergraduates were $450 at Oklahoma and $1200 at Hopkins. Medical students could expect to spend an average of $925 each year.[27]

A recurrent criticism of two years of college preparation as a requirement of admission to medical school was that it would eliminate opportunities for the poor boy. Not so, declared Dr. N. P. Colwell, secretary of the Council on Medical Education. In 1923, he found "opportunities were even more numerous than anticipated."[28] After surveying fifty universites and colleges, Colwell discovered that between 50 and 65 percent of the students earned part of their expenses and 15 to 20 percent were totally self-supporting. Medical schools, he admitted, presented more of a problem because of the shortage of spare time and the meager job offerings. Still some students (he did not say how many) supported themselves all the way through medical school, and there were always summer jobs and loans.[29] For the best students, forth-six medical schools offered more than five hundred scholarships, which usually paid tuition but not much more.[30]

Financing a medical education was difficult for any student but particularly so for women because they had fewer opportunities for self-support or to secure scholarships. While 46 percent of the male undergraduates earned part of their expenses in 1927-1928, only 25 percent of the females did. At coeducational schools, 25 percent of the men and 14 percent of the women were totally self-supporting. Women's colleges, which supplied a disproportionate number of women medical students, generally had a higher average tuition and a lower percentage of self-help students than either men's or coeducational schools.[31]   On the average, women students earned less than their brothers.   .Women students also had fewer chances for scholarships than men did.   A survey of the scholarships available in 1927-1928 showed that 3,122 were restricted to women, 9,685 were restricted to men, and 21,206 were open to both sexes.   The schools awarded scholarships to 8,834 women and 21,168 men.   Of the 747 scholarships awarded for all levels of medical education that year, women received fity-two (7 percent), most of which covered only tuition.[32]   Dr. Colwell may have reflected the Council's lack of concern with the problem of females in medical education when he casually remarked that "girls teach in the summer and do tutoring in their spare time in the winter," to supplement their funds.   Neither could have produced much income.[33]   Despite the impressive increases in female college enrollment during the twenties, higher education for women was clearly a luxury limited largely to the upper classes.   The additional cost of medical school was even more restrictive.   Indeed, when Dr. Florence Brown Sherbon, President of the Kansas Medical Women's Association, asked a college audience why more women were not planning careers in medicine, the high cost of medical education was cited as a major deterrent.[34]

Despite its costliness in time, money, and energy, medicine gained in popularity as a career: not only enrollment but also applications rose steadily during the twenties.   Yet each fall, schools had empty places in their freshman classes.   Officials realized that their announcements about limiting the size of classes had triggered a state of panic among interested students who reacted by sending out multiple applications.[35]   It was a growing phenomenon: 10,006 individuals submitted 20,093 applications in 1926, but 13,655 students sent out 31,749 applications in 1930.   The number of students accepted was 6,420 in 1926 and 7,035 in 1930.   It was not unusual for a student to submit thirty or more applications.   Women were less prone to panic, apparently, because they applied an average of 1.6 times to men's average of 2.3 times.[36]

As competition to get into medical school heightened, school administrators reflected on the task and opportunities confronting them. Dr. Burton D. Meyers, Dean of the Indiana University Medical School, analyzed the applications and commented:

> The schools of medicine of America occupy a position that is unique—unprecedented.   No other school of any university is forced by applications greatly exceeding school capacity to select so discriminatingly the membership of its classes.[37]

Meyers regarded this fortuitous situation as a means of eliminating the waste of accepting mediocre students who would never graduate. The problem was trying to determine which students would complete the program. Without even the rough guidance provided by aptitude tests, officials relied on grades, quality of undergraduate training, and recommendations. Students sought to improve their chances for acceptance by submitting credentials showing more than the minimum requirements. The strategy worked, too. Of the matriculants in 1929, 45 percent had bachelor's degrees and 49 percent had four years of college credits. Nineteen medical colleges did not admit any students presenting just two years of college preparation although six of these schools specified two years as their mimimum requirement.[38]   Johns Hopkins, one of the two institutions to demand a baccalaureate, adopted a policy in 1925 of taking only the very best students from the very best colleges and requiring a personal interview and a deposit of $25 from each applicant. Officials expected that they would not fill their seventy-five spaces for several years and were, therefore, surprised in 1927 to have over one hundred exceptionally good applications from which to select their first-year class.[39]   Because Hopkins substantially reduced its attrition rate by this means, other schools considered adopting a similar policy.

Clearly, the method of selecting medical students provided wide latitude for discrimination against particular groups. And yet, Dr. Meyers declared, if there was any discrimination, it was in favor of women. Between 1926 and 1929, women composed 4.4 percent of the applicants and 4.6 percent of the acceptances. During this period, 60 percent of the females and 56 percent of the males were admitted. The discrepancy appeared to be growing because women made up 3.5 of the applicants and 4.4 percent of the acceptances in 1929; 65 percent of the female applicants but only 51 percent of the males were admitted.[40]   To a certain extent, the result reflected the inflated number of men choosing medicine as a career: the number of women applicants simply did not grow as rapidly as the number of male applicants. Yet Meyers was incorrect in his conclusion that women received preferential treatment because, as a group, they submitted better applications than their male competitors did. Meyers himself recognized this fact: "We are probably justified in assuming that a higher percentage of women who present themselves for matriculation in medical schools are well prepared for the study of medicine.[41]

As a group, medical schools did not pursue a coordinated policy of discrimination against women applicants: there was no 5 percent quota. In some schools, women usually made up 10 percent of the student body. This group included Johns Hopkins, Columbia University, the University of Chicago, and Cornell University—all highly rated schools.[42]   Other medical colleges, however, had few or no female students throughout the twenties, indicating that discrimination probably existed on an individual basis. In a survey of coeducational institutions at the end of the decade, Dr. Bertha Van Hoosen, junior editor of the *Medical Woman's Journal,* found several school officials who were reluctant to admit women because they thought, but never substantiated with concrete statistics, that large numbers of women dropped out of medicine. One administrator erroneously assumed that fifty percent of the women students quit medical school and therefore females were twice as expensive as males to train. Another official saw no problem "'as long as we can keep the number of women students within limits.'"[43] The usual method of "keeping the number within limits" involved different standards for male and female applicants: women were expected to exhibit better credentials and more dedication than men.[44]

Little clear-cut evidence has emerged to show how women performed in medical schools during the twenties. One study of the University of Michigan medical school showed that women students, on the average, were better prepared and made higher grades than their male counterparts did.[45] The sample was extremely small and covered only the earliest years of the decade. Dr. Van Hoosen had reports from over forty coeducational medical colleges that indicated that women equalled men as medical students.[46] Since the competition to get into medical school grew and school officials became increasingly selective, it would seem likely that the women were good students and performed creditably. Enrollment figures for women at individual schools fluctuated widely from year to year, indicating that women dropped out, transferred, or came back. The evidence did not show conclusively that women had a higher rate of attrition than men.[47] Because the number of male students grew more rapidly than that of women, the proportion of females in the student body decreased as the decade wore on. Yet the method of selection and the competition involved suggests that the young women pursuing medical careers were in all likelihood a competent group.

If a woman could not afford the time and expense of medical education, law offered many possibilities for professional training. To become a lawyer in any state in 1920, it was not necessary to attend college or even law school. No state specified the length of time to be spent in the study of the law for licensure.[48] A woman could choose between reading law in an office or attending any of the 102 schools which offered a variety of course lengths, admission requirements, meeting times, and tuitions.[49]   Unlike their sisters in medicine, women who wanted to become attorneys could work full-time during the day and earn law degrees at night.

Women took advantage of the educational opportunities opening to them in the twenties. The number of female law students rose from 1,166 in 1920 to 2,203 in 1930 and composed between 5 and 6 percent of the law student population each year.[50]   At least twice as many women studied law as studied medicine.   There was a catch, however.   As newcomers, they had pioneer roles, and the vocational literature echoed a familiar theme:

> In the present development of the profession and in view of the handicaps she still carries, no woman can afford to enter law with inadequate preparation.   She should in every case plan for the very best training possible, which means not only the very best law course but a fundamental cultural education underlying it.[51]

While some women followed this sage advice, the majority of women pursuing a legal degree either did not or could not. They took advantage of part-time programs that required less in terms of tuition, time, and sacrifices than the full-time schools.

The conditions that enabled women to obtain legal training and admission to the bar—part-time and off-hour courses—were precisely the ones that the American Bar Association and the Association of American Law Schools wanted to eliminate.   Under existing procedures and requirements, far too many incompetents and, more to the point, far too many members of the lower and immigrant classes were joining the profession.[52]   Leaders of the ABA and the AALS, impressed by the success of the medical profession in eliminating proprietary schools while improving medical education, decided to duplicate the physicians' plan of action. The ABA had commissioned the Carnegie Foundation to study law schools in the manner Flexner had surveyed medical colleges and had established a Council on Legal Education to implement he expected recommendations.   Alfred Z. Reed, the man chosen for the job, would follow in Flexner's footsteps and suggest upgrading the standards for education and admission to the profession and the elimination of the part-time schools.

When Reed's work, *Training for the Public Profession of the Law,* appeared in 1921, it corroborated some of the ideas of the reformers but not all.   Reed agreed that part-time schools, in their current condition, hurt the profession. The night schools attempted to duplicate a full-time curriculum in a truncated course; it was impossible for part-time students to learn as much law as those devoting substantially all their time to their studies.[53]   But Reed saw nothing incurably wrong with night schools, provided they improved. Their growth, he said, was a "healthy and desirable" phenomenon:

> Humanitarian and political considerations unite in leading us to approve of efforts to widen the circle of those who are able to study the law. The organization of educational machinery is especially designed to abolish economic handicaps—intended to place the poor boy, so far as possible, on an equal footing with the rich—constitutes one of America's fundamental ideals.[54]

A layman, Reed examined the profession from the point of view of what society needed. Law was a public profession intimately bound up with the making of laws and the administration of justice. Not all law students become, or even intend to become attorneys. Not all lawyers provide the same service or have the same clientele. Under the circumstances, Reed wrote, it was ridiculous to impose the same curriculum and requirements for licensure on all students. The proposed standards would not filter out the unfit or necessarily improve legal services. Reed suggested institutionalizing the existing diversity within the profession by having a stratified bar divided along educational lines.[55]

Proponents of higher standards were not impressed with the Reed Report. The response of Harlan J. Stone, Dean of Columbia University Law School, was typical. He attacked the Report as the product of an ignorant outsider and then launched into a tirade against Reed's suggestion to improve part-time schools:

> From this follows, apparently, the conclusion . . . that the low grade law school is justified and should be cherished and protected and consequently that the low grade bar examination is likewise justified and should be protected, since with the prevailing standards of education and popular intelligence it is only by the preservation of these standards and methods that the way can be kept open for the great bulk of our population to enter the bar.[56]

Dean Stone misinterpreted Reed's recommendation: Reed did not want to maintain low standards but to differentiate between levels of competence and service.[57]

The Reed Report and the proposal to establish higher educational standards were the focus of the annual convention of the ABA in 1921. After a heated debate in which representatives of the prominent law firms and the AALS argued for and representatives of part-time schools and rural bar associations argued against higher standards, Joseph S. Dickey, a lawyer from Texas, rose to address the meeting:

> I'm sick and tired of having doctors, dentists, preachers, chiropractors, and others boast that only educated men can join their profession, but that it takes no great amount of learning to be a lawyer. . . . I still believe that the law is a learned profession; I still believe that in the long run it takes an educated man to succeed at the bar, and it is almost criminal to encourage the uneducated man with promises of success.[58]

The appeal to professional pride tipped the scales in favor of higher standards, and the resolutions were adopted by the ABA.

In some respects, the ABA resolutions were compromises which met even Reed's approval.[59] The ABA did not rule out the possibility of attending part-time schools if the courses were longer and the institution met the other requirements for accreditation. For approval, schools needed an adequate library, full-time faculty, and entrance requirements of at least two years of college credits. The ABA recommended that only graduates of accredited schools be allowed to take the bar exam.[60] Like the AMA, the ABA had no legal authority to force schools to adopt the new rules. Consequently, the leaders of the ABA invited representatives from local and state bar associations to a Conference on Legal Education to persuade them to use their influence on the appropriate authorities in their home states.

If the proponents of higher standards expected the ABA resolutions to end the controversy, they were doomed to disappointment: it continued throughout the decade. Reformers refused to believe there was anything good to be said about part-time schools and their graduates, and opponents saw the movement for higher standards as a plutocratic plot against the poor boy.[61] One fact appeared clear in the early twenties: women did not figure in the debate either as participants or as an allegedly objectionable group. In his Report, Reed wrote that women presented no problem to the profession and added in a footnote: "Space does not permit an account of this movement [of women into the profession] which has produced much less momentous results than were anticipated by either its advocates or its opponents."[62] In all his many articles and reports on the legal profession during the twenties, Reed never did find space to discuss women attorneys. He apparently considered their impact negligible, a view apparently shared by many lawyers, since comments on women were noticeably absent from the professional journals.

While factions within the profession debated the pros and cons of higher standards, some schools began adopting the guidelines established by the ABA. The first list of schools accredited by the ABA appeared in 1923 and contained thirty-nine Class A and nine Class B institutions. Within a year, four universities dropped their evening or part-time divisions and several other schools announced their intention of raising their admissions requirements. The list of approved law schools grew to sixty-one in 1926 and to seventy-one by 1930.[63]

A few schools went beyond the minimum standards set by the ABA. The two-year college requirement did not always weed out those unsuited to legal study, and attrition rates were sometimes as high as 35 percent. Officials added more years of college work to their entrance standards in hopes of cutting attrition. By 1924, six law schools demanded or had announced a new policy of accepting only those students with bachelor's degrees.[64] At about the same time, several institutions began experimenting with law aptitude tests. Yale was first, in 1927, to use the test, along with interviews, grades, and recommendations, as a means of selecting and restricting its incoming classes. When Yale's attrition rate dropped, other prominent schools followed its example.[65]

Although the number of accredited schools grew annually, their progress was overshadowed by the explosion of part-time schools. Between 1920 and 1928, the number of exclusively full-time institutions rose from seventy to seventy-seven; those offering mixed programs (both full and part-time courses) increased from eight to twenty; and strictly part-time schools grew from seventy-two to seventy-nine. Between 1920 and 1926, enrollment increased by 26.7 percent in full-time schools, 31.4 percent in part-time institutions, and 312.4 percent in mixed schools. The proportion of law students in full-time courses thus actually decreased over the decade.[66]

The reasons for the steady growth of part-time law courses were not difficult to find. Despite the propaganda of the ABA, few states had increased their requirements for admission to the bar. In 1928, only five states demanded two years of college training, and only fifteen required a high school diploma. Although thirty-one states specified three years of legal training, only one said it must be at a law school. As yet, no state required graduation from a law school, and only thirty-five demanded examination by a public authority.[67] The admissions policies of the states provided little incentive for students to secure a thorough education or for law schools to upgrade their programs.

Another factor affecting a prospective student's choice of schools was cost. President James Angell of Yale seriously doubted whether the students of the lower classes could afford tuition of both undergraduate and law schools.[68] The annual tuition at accredited law schools attached to state universities ranged from $30 at the University of Texas to $230 at the University of Virginia, but Harvard, Columbia, and Yale charged over $300 and the University of Pennsylvania charged $400. Unlike medical schools, very few law schools had scholarships for worthy students. In contrast, non-accredited part-time law schools rarely cost more than $150 per year and frequently considerably less.[69] An added advantage of night schools was that they did not prohibit the student from working full-time during the day.

The policies adopted by accredited law schools and the cost of tuition affected women students as well as men. While most law schools, accredited and non-accredited, accepted women by the mid-twenties, female representation was disproportionately low in the former. Women composed between 5 and 6 percent of all law students and between 4.5 and 6 percent of all graduates during the twenties. But they only made up between 2.5 and 4 percent of the students and between 2 and 3 percent of the graduates of accredited schools. While the proportion of male students who studied at approved institutions fell from 42.6 percent in 1920 to 32.7 percent in 1930, the proportion of female declined from 32.7 percent to 23.7 percent.[70] The number of accredited law schools admitting women had grown over the years, but the number and proportion of their female students remained small.

That approved schools discriminated against women applicants seems almost certain: they had shown greater reluctance than part-time schools in accepting women in the first place. But certainly economic and educational factors played a part in each woman's decision to attend a particular school. Beatrice Doerschuk's study, *Women in the Law,* revealed that a large number of the women in her sample had worked prior to or during the time they studied law, most frequently as clerical workers or teachers. The majority attended part-time courses because of financial reasons or discrimination.[71] The Portia School of Law in Boston and the Washington College of Law in the District of Columbia were founded specifically for women, though the latter had become coeducational by the twenties. A large portion of the women who attended each institution were clerical workers.[72] The annual wages of a secretary or stenographer ranged from $750 to $1500, low enough to preclude their attending a full-time law course without financial assistance. It was also unlikely that many such marginally paid clerical workers could have met the educational requirements of two years of college credits.

Women, along with other groups, benefited from the variety of educational opportunities in law. Almost anyone could obtain some kind of legal training, a fact which created some problems. The attrition rate for law schools was unusually high. For all law schools, the loss of enrollment between the first and second years fluctuated between 18 and 30 percent, and the loss between the first and the third year ranged from 29 to 43 percent. It was not unusual for Harvard or Columbia to lose a third of their first-year students, but the same was true of part-time schools such as the John Marshall School of Law in Chicago.[73] Undoubtedly, poor scholarship and laziness accounted for part of the drop-out rate. Many students, however, quit law school as soon as they had attained the minimum requirements or knowledge needed to pass the bar exams. The results of the state bar exams illustrated with devastating clarity the failure of the training system and of the students to take advantage of existing educational opportunities: quite frequently, 60 percent of the candidates in a state would fail in any given year.[74]

Another reason for the high rate of failure on bar exams was that in some states the tests were used to weed out the undesirable groups of candidates when the educational system did not. One method adopted by several states was the introduction of the character test, a vague concept that apparently included a person's morals and conduct and, sometimes, his ethnic background. In Ohio in 1923, five disbarment cases (one of which was a woman) just prior to the bar exam sent officials scurrying to find out about the history, character, and conduct of all 503 candidates. Lawyer, Ellahue A. Harper, reported the results of the inquiry:

> Among this greater number of applicants one-half were from Cleveland alone and of this quota from Cleveland the majority were foreigners. The court decided on the face of things many of them were undesirable. . . . As a consequence many of the 60% of the failures for that year were the result of those fifteen hundred and nine letters. Some were failed even before their papers containing answers to questions were looked over. The letters in these instances did not contain information satisfactory to the committee. One man who failed protested and wanted to know whether he answered the questions correctly. He was told that his papers were well up near the top in excellence. He asked why he was not passed, and was told his character was too poor.[75]

Ohio apparently had not used a character test prior to that time. New York and New Jersey both had high concentrations of first and second generation Americans and part-time law students taking bar exams. They also had strict character tests for candidates and usually failed about 50 percent of the applicants.[76]   One cannot but wonder if they failed because of poor training or because of discrimination. Since the statistics for bar exams were not broken down according to sex, it is impossible to tell whether the same tactics were employed against women.

If male lawyers had been reticent about women joining the profession in the early twenties, by the end of the decade they had begun voicing their opinions.   In 1927, The *American Law School Review* reported a debate held by the New York Bar Association on a proposal to raise the educational prerequisites to three years of college work and quoted one Mr. Alan Fox:

> The girl applicants have presented a vexing problem. There are now a good many of them. There is no intrinsic reason that I know of why girls should not make competent lawyers, but those who have applied for admission this year have been with few exceptions of very inferior quality. Most of them have been stenographers from the small law offices who have taken night law courses. . . . Most of them clearly can never become competent lawyers. . . .[77]

Miss Lewinson, a product of a night law course and the representative of the Women Lawyers' Association of New York at the debate, objected to Fox's remarks as being ill-informed and exaggerated.   Miss Lewinson pointed out that stenographers took law courses to improve their salaries as clerical workers, not to become lawyers. Of the women attorneys she had personally helped place in law offices, 30 percent had college degrees.[78]

Despite the favorable record made by women, the idea of a female menace persisted in some corners of the profession. By 1929, many attorneys complained about the the over-crowded condition of the profession and clamored for yet higher standards as a means of curtailing numbers. Women lawyers received a part of the blame. A law professor from Fordham University, I. Maurice Wormser, had championed the right of the poor boy to improve himself through a law career at the beginning of the decade, but he deplored the influx of women lawyers:

> Last but not least, we are faced with an ever growing influx of Portias, some of whom are remarkably efficient and all of whom are willing to work for excessively low wages.[79]

Wormser castigated women attorneys along with all those others such as corporations, foreigners, and trust companies which he saw as usurping the legitimate business of male lawyers. Thus by the end of the decade, women had fallen into the group of individuals that some lawyers wished to see kept to a minimum.

Although the ABA tried to eliminate proprietary schools, educational opportunities in law did expand during the twenties, and women, along with other groups, took advantage of them. But unlike medical women who concentrated in the better schools, women law students gravitated toward non-accredited, part-time courses. Male students did, too, but not to the same extent that women did. While such institutions provided access to the legal profession, the education a woman received would influence the kind of position she obtained later.

Unlike physicians and attorneys, educators did not spend their time trying to exclude certain groups of individuals from the profession but sought ways to lure young men and women into college teaching. During the twenties, higher education experienced its greatest growth since the Commissioner of Education first published data on colleges in 1870. Undergraduate enrollment rose 121 percent from 341,082 to 753,827, and the Bureau of Education reported the addition of 183 four-year colleges and professional schools and 225 new junior colleges.[80] The female segment of the enrollment grew most rapidly: it increased by 142 percent while the male enrollment rose 108 percent. At the same time, the number of graduate students and Ph.D. recipients surged upward. Registration in graduate programs increased by 297.4 percent with the addition of 42,849 students and new doctorates rose by 267.4 percent. A total of 13,947 persons received their Ph.D. during the decade, and women made up 15.2 percent of the group.[81] Not only was there, for a time, an abundance of positions in college teaching, but also more men and women than ever before were obtaining the most thorough training available for those positions.

Despite the impressive expansion of higher education, leaders in the field felt themselves at a distinct disadvantage. In his annual report, President Shurman of Cornell University summed up the problems facing the academic profession:

> There has never been a time when it was so difficult to secure first-class men, and especially young men, to fill university positions. . . . Young men of superior parts. . .are deterred from entering the profession by an aversion to the drudgery of teaching mediocre students and by a lack of time and opportunity offered for independent scholarship or scientific research. There is also the competition of other professions, and especially, in these days, of business, in which the universities are at a great financial disadvantage.[82]

Educators thought that the profession offered few inducements to prospective recruits. Salaries, particularly in comparison to the fees of doctors and lawyers, were low and had not kept pace with inflation. A study of 182 institutions revealed that in 1920 the average salary for an instructor was $1,393, 27 percent more than he received in 1912-1913; full professors received $2,628, an increase of 6.5 percent. It was estimated, however, that the cost of living had doubled in the same period.[83] As employees of colleges and universities, faculty members had few opportunities to improve their economic status.

Academicians worried about what would become of their profession because they were competing for the bright young men. In 1927, Frederick A. Ogg reported that there were 999 independent research laboratories in the United States which lured trained individuals from academia. Business and industry provided positions for scientists, statisticians, and sociologists, and the government also competed for scholars. So severe had the situation become by 1928, warned Ogg, that universities, the traditional source of science and scholarship, were in danger of being seriously depleted.[84] Research positions often had attractive incomes and a higher social status than academic positions enjoyed.

The academic profession operated under a special set of factors that differed radically from those affecting the legal and medical professions. College teachers were not self-employed and therefore had less control over their working lives than was true with independent lawyers or doctors. There was also the problem of multiple loyalties: who, or what, was the "client"—the student, the university, or society? Were academicians members, first and foremost, of the teaching profession, of a university, or of a discipline? The conflicts prevented college teachers from developing as clearly defined a sense of professional identity as either doctors or lawyers had during the twenties.[85] By the same token, teachers had less control over their profession than the other two groups had. The American Association of University Professors (AAUP) did not set the standards for training: they were established and monitored by outside organizations such as accrediting agencies, state legislatures, the Carnegie Foundation, professional schools, and the AAU.[86] No formal licensing procedure existed with which academicians could control the number and quality of the entrants. Clearly, teachers could not rely on the same tactics that doctors and lawyers had used to improve their profession.

Although the AAUP discussed endlessly the kind of training teachers ought to have, the organization did not tamper with the existing system during the twenties. The only branch of the profession to discuss seriously the limiting of enrollment or of using a more rigorous selection process was the AAU, and that organization never went beyond discussion either. Yet this non-policy, as much as the plans and programs of the AMA or the ABA, affected the prospective educators of both sexes.

The number of men and women attending graduate school grew markedly during the decade, and more individuals earned Ph.D.'s during the twenties than in the previous four decades combined.[87] Undoubtedly the rise was related to the expansion of college education both because it supplied qualified students for graduate programs and because it created a demand for trained personnel to teach larger classes. The standards imposed by accrediting agencies encouraged institutions to hire instructors with advanced degrees.

Certain advantages attached to graduate education outweighed its negative aspects. The main prerequisite for entrance was graduation from an approved undergraduate school, and the entire process of obtaining a Master's or a Doctor's degree could be a long and costly ordeal. But a student could interrupt the process to earn money for tuition and fees. Nor was it unusual for an individual to start his formal career without the degree in hand, whereas both medicine and law required a license before entering practice. In the 1920's, the total average time-lapse between graduation from college and receipt of the Ph.D. was 8.4 years, indicating that many doctoral candidates did interrupt their training. At the same time, scholarships and fellowships eased the way for a minority of students. In 1927-28, the Bureau of Education listed 1,793 fellowships awarded in more than fifty disciplines providing financial assistance to 4 percent of the graduate student body.[88] While many were limited to tuition for only a year or two, other scholarships covered living expenses as well as lasted for several years. It appeared that fellowships helped to shorten the time it took to earn a Ph.D. Two of the best funded fields, chemistry and engineering, also had the two shortest averages for time-lapse between bachelor's and doctor's degrees.[89]

The potential for future employment and the opportunities within graduate schools attracted women as well as men. By the 1920's, some graduate programs still granted few or no Ph.D.'s to women. But the elite schools—Chicago, Columbia, Cornell, Yale, and Radcliffe (the female branch of Harvard graduate school)—all had sizeable enrollments. In fact, they accounted for 40 percent of the Ph.D.'s awarded to women during the twenties.[90]

Women had more difficulty obtaining financial aid than getting into graduate schools. In 1928, although they made up nearly 40 percent of all graduate students, women received only 14.6 percent of the fellowships awarded that year.   While 5.8 percent of all male graduate students obtained financial aid, only 1.4 percent of the females did.[91] Women found their chances better in certain disciplines. They received all of the fellowships in home economics, 63 percent of those in hygiene and public health, 50 percent of those in psychology, German, and botany, and 47 percent of those in sociology. Out of the 197 fellowships in various kinds of engineering, however, only one went to a woman. In general, women were more likely to receive economic assistance in fields where they were heavily represented or predominated. The only major exception was education, where women received only 15 percent of the fellowships in 1928.[92]

As was true of male graduate students, many women delayed commencement of their advanced education or interrupted it. A survey made by the American Association of University Women (AAUW) of a thousand women who received their doctorates before June, 1924 showed that the median time lapse between bachelor's and doctoral degrees was about eight years, which was typical of all graduate students. Although 70 percent of the respondents had obtained fellowships, most had found it necessary to supplement their funds with either part-time or full-time jobs.[93] Women concentrated more heavily in fields with longer than average time-lapses—social sciences, arts, and education—than in either the physical or biological sciences, which had shorter average time-lapses.[94] It was also true that the fields with the most funds available for scholarships and fellowships were the natural sciences.

The amount of money available for any discipline reflected its prestige and relative ranking and its supposed value to society. Science, particularly chemistry, engineering, and medicine ranked high, while modern language, art, and music ranked low. In between were the social sciences and education.[95] Women were poorly represented in the prestige fields in terms of number of graduate students and of fellowship recipients. Personal inclination accounted partly for the distribution of women, but discrimination played a role as well. In the field of chemistry, for example, commercial firms often financed the education of future employees. The attitude of company executives toward women in the field was often negative. Mr. N. B. Davis of the Cincinnati Chemical Company, for example, wrote, "I see no future for women in chemistry. As far as I am aware, there are not five successful women chemists in the United States."[96] Davis' sentiments were shared by Hugh K. Moore of the Brown Company in Berlin, New Hampshire: "In doing work a woman stenographer is bad enough, but a woman chemist is impossible."[97] Davis and Moore were not isolated examples in the field of chemistry, and it was not surprising that women received only thirteen out of 149 fellowships awarded in 1927-1928.[98] A practical woman might have preferred to devote herself to a discipline where the animosity to her sex was less pronounced and the possibilities for future employment more assured.

Not all doctorates became college teachers, nor did all professors hold the Ph.D. during the twenties, two circumstances which probably increased employment opportunities for women. If industry, government, and private research organizations siphoned off trained personnel from the academic labor pool, as Frederick A. Ogg's study suggested, it meant that positions became vacant in college teaching. The existence of research in fields outside of universities also presented women with alternative means of employment.

Despite the premium placed on advanced degrees, not all college teachers possessed them. During the decade, graduate schools produced 13,947 Ph.D.'s while the number of college teachers rose by 26,082. The number of women teachers more than doubled with the addition of 7,991 recruits, but only 2,127 women earned doctorates.[99] The North Central 'Association, one of the major accrediting agencies, confirmed the fact that it was possible for individuals to secure positions without advanced degrees. The NCA surveyed the training of 8,743 teachers in its member schools in 1928 and found numerous violations of its standards. A baccalaureate was a prerequisite for all faculty members, but 215 teachers, primarily part-time instructors and members of physical education departments, did not possess the degree. Full-time professors were expected to have at least a Master's degree or equivalent technical training, but over 12 percent of the members of this category did not. Department heads were supposed to have Ph.D.'s, but slightly less than half of the chairmen met this requirement. Only 55 percent of the faculty members at institutions accredited by the NCA had Master's degrees.[100]

An advanced degree, although a definite advantage, was not essential for getting into college teaching. The rapid expansion of higher education created a demand for instructors, and graduate schools responded by enlarging their programs and producing ever greater numbers of degree candidates and recipients. More women than ever before attended graduate schools, earned advanced degrees, and joined faculties. In comparison to men, however, a smaller proportion of women possessed M.A.'s and Ph.D.'s, a fact which would affect their later careers.

Since education and training provided the main entries into medicine, law, and higher education during the twenties, the change in policies, in operation with other factors, helped determine how many women joined each occupation. In all three fields, the number and proportion of professional schools admitting women grew during the decade. The AMA refined its policy of maintaining high standards and eliminating inferior schools, while the ABA tried, with only limited success, to copy its example. The academic profession, which had very little control over the training of future teachers, made no attempt to alter the system. Although the policies, or non-policies, were not anti-female in intent, women were nevertheless affected by the changes. In each case, however, the results were different.

In medicine, students of both sexes not only met the high requirements but went beyond them as competition to get into medical school stiffened. The statistics are incomplete, but it appears that the number of women applicants grew more slowly than the number of male applicants. Perhaps women did not wish to compete, or, as Dr. Martha Tracy, Dean of the Women's Medical College suggested, they may not have had access to information early enough in their educational careers to fulfill the prerequisites.[101] Or economic considerations may have played a part. The cost of medical education doubled during the decade, and the prospect of remaining income-less for six to nine years may have deterred many women or their parents.[102] From the scanty evidence available, it would appear that the women who did go to medical school probably came from the upper classes: a disproportionate number attended eastern women's colleges which had high tuition and very few self-help students, and they gravitated toward some of the more expensive medical colleges.[103] It was also true that, as a group, women applicants submitted better credentials than their male competitors. Despite the small size of the female population in medical schools, they were probably a very competent group.

In comparison to their sisters in medicine and teaching, women made a late start in the legal profession, but they nevertheless took advantage of the widening opportunities for legal education. Because the ABA failed to impose its standards on all law schools during the 1920's, part-time schools, with their flexible schedules, low tuition, and minimum entrance requirements, flourished. Despite much advice to attend only accredited law schools, women concentrated in the part-time schools. Probably the welcome extended to women by approved schools was lukewarm at best. The evidence suggests, however, that many of the female law students were former clerical workers who could not meet the educational or financial requirements of quality law schools. While many of these women probably did not intend to practice law, those who did were receiving an education that the leaders of the profession considered to be inferior. Naturally, this would affect a woman's chances for future employment.

Of the three professions, higher education presented the fewest obstacles. Women had composed a larger proportion of college teachers than of either physicians or lawyers since before the turn of the century. The rapid expansion of higher education during the twenties, particularly of female enrollment, created a demand for teachers. Unlike the AMA or the ABA, the AAUP had little control over the training and production of future teachers, and it did not attempt to impose new educational standards on graduate schools that might have curtailed enrollment. More women attended graduate schools than attended medical or law schools, and more women entered teaching than entered medicine or law. It was not necessary to have an advanced degree to become a college instructor, and many women did not have one. On the surface, the situation in higher education appeared beneficial for women.

Superficially, the opportunities for women to secure advanced training had grown during the twenties as more schools opened their doors to them. But for a woman the decision to follow a professional career involved more than choosing a training program. A woman had to consider the financial burden, the years spent in preparation, the selection of a speciality, and the delay, if not elimination, of personal plans concerning marriage. The decision did not appear to become any easier to make as the decade wore on.

NOTES

[1]Each year in August, JAMA published statistics and information on the medical schools in the United States and Canada. The "Education Number," as it was called, provided the best information on professional students of all three fields under consideration. The usual title of the article was "Medical Education in the United States," but in this paper it will be referred to as the "Medical Education Number." "Medical Education Number, 1920," *JAMA* 75 (August 7, 1920), 379; U. S., Department of the Interior, Bureau of Education, "Biennial Survey of Education: Statistics of Universities, Colleges, and Professional Schools, 1919-1920," *Bulletin*, No. 28 (1922), 5 (hereafter cited as "Biennial Survey of Education"); See Tables 1, 3, and 5 in the Appendix fo "Biennial Survey of Education"); See Tables 1, 3, and 5 in the Appendix for summaries of enrollment in all three fields.

[2]Harry H. Moore, "Health and Medical Practice," in President's Research Committee on Social Trends, *Recent Social Trends in the United States* (New York: McGraw-Hill, 1933), 1061-1072.

[3]Charles E. Clark and William O. Douglas, "Law and Legal Institutions," in *Recent Social Trends in the United States*, 1448-1453.

[4]"Biennial Survey of Education, 1917-1918," 6-8; "Biennial Survey of Education, 1919-1920," 5.

[5]T. J. O'Donnell, "Has the Lawyer Lost Caste?" *Central Law Journal* 91 (September 24, 1920), 227.

[6]George Gray Ward, Jr., "Relation of the Medical Profession to the Community," *Medical Record* 99 (February 26, 1921), 337.

[7]O'Donnell, 226; I. Maurice Wormser, "Fewer Lawyers and Better Ones," *American Bar Association Journal* 15 (April, 1929), 207-208 (hereafter cited as *ABAJ*); Jules Henry Cohen, "Lay Practice of Law Injures Clients, Not Legal Profession," *Journal of the American Judicature Society* 5 (August, 1929), 52-53.

[8]Arthur O. Lovejoy, "Annual Message of the President," *AAUP Bulletin* 5 (November-December, 1919), 17-20.

[9]The *AAUP Bulletin*, the *Bulletin of the Association of American Medical Colleges* (cited hereafter as *AAMC Bulletin*), and the *American Law School Review* (cited hereafter as *ALSR*) carried on discussion about the topic throughout the decade. Significantly, the discussions were always couched in terms of attracting the best young men rather than of attracting the best young men and women.

[10]See Table 1 in the Appendix.

[11]Charles F. Painter, "Educational Requirements for the Twentieth Century Practice," *Boston Medical and Surgical Journal* 194 (June 10, 1926), 1064.

[12]John M. Giles, "Medical Education and Medical Supply," *Boston Medical and Surgical Journal* 185 (September 29, 1921), 289-390.

[13]Raymond Pearl, "Distribution of Physicians in the United States," *JAMA* 84 (April 4, 1925), 1024-1026.

[14]U. S., Department of the Interior, Bureau of Education, *Opportunities for the Study of Medicine in the United States,* by George Frederick Zook (Washington, D.C.: Government Printing Office, 1920), 1, 11.

[15]See the "Medical Education Numbers" for the years 1920-1930.

[16]Ibid.

[17]"State Board Statistics for 1920," *JAMA* 76 (April 30, 1921), 1239; "State Board Statistics for 1927," *JAMA* 90 (May 5, 1928), 1212.

[18]"State Board Statistics for 1928," *JAMA* 92 (April 27, 1929), 1431.

[19]Both men and women who had bachelor's degrees performed better than students without degrees. A. C. Curtis, "Women as Students of Medicine," *AAMC Bulletin* 2 (April, 1927), 140-148.

[20]In 1929, two schools demanded baccalaureates, thirteen required ninety college credits (three years), and three required seventy-two credits. F. C. Zapffe, "Analysis of Entrance Credentials Presented by Freshmen Admitted in 1929," *Journal of the Association of American Medical Colleges* 5 (July, 1930), 231 (Hereafter cited as *AAMC Journal);* F. D. Baker, "Determining the Fitness of Premedical Students," *AAMC Bulletin* 2 (January, 1927), 16-21.

[21]N. P. Colwell, "Present Needs in Medical Education," *JAMA* 82 (March 15, 1924), 839.

[22]U. S., Department of the Interior, Bureau of Education, "Medical Education, 1918-1920," *Bulletin,* No. 15 (1921), 15, 10; "Medical Education Number, 1930," *JAMA* 95 (August 16, 1930), 487-534.

[23]Because there were six hospitals in 1920 and 1930 that took only female interns, there were actually enought slots for all women graduates. See "Medical Education Number, 1920," 409-414; "Medical Education Number, 1930," 517-534.

[24]It should be noted that not all students had their degrees when they began medical school. Some students were enrolled in a combined undergraduate-medical program and others earned their degrees while in medical school during the summer. "Medical Education Number, 1930," 504.

[25]"Medical Education Number, 1930," 504.

[26]"Medical Education Number, 1920," 380-382; "Medical Education Number, 1930," 500-501; "Biennial Survey of Education, 1919-1920," 106-125; U.S., Department of the Interior, Bureau of Education, "Self-Help for College Students," *Bulletin,* No. 2 (1929), 75-134; Huber W. Hurt listed the tuition for the two undergraduate schools as being the same in 1933 as in 1928, therefore we may assume the tuition was the same in 1930. Huber William Hurt, *The College Blue Book* (Holleywood-by-the-Sea, Fla: College Blue Book, 1933), 78, 114.

[27]"Self-Help for College Students," 1.

[28]N. P. Colwell, "Can the Poor Boy Secure a Medical Education?" *JAMA* 81 (August 8, 1923), 577.

[29]Ibid., 577, 578.

[30]See the "Medical Education Numbers," for the years 1920-1930; U. S., Department of the Interior, Bureau of Education, "Scholarships and Fellowships: Grants Available in United States Colleges and Universities," *Bulletin*, No. 15 (1931), 93-96.

[31]"Self-Help for College Students," 58-61; In 1929, 113 medical students came from women's colleges and fifty-nine of those came from eight eastern women's colleges. See "Medical Education Number, 1930," 488-496; "Question of Women's Colleges," *Atlantic Monthly* 140 (November, 1927), 582.

[32]"Scholarships and Fellowships," 93-96.

[33]Colwell, "Can the Poor Boy. . .," 577.

[34]Florence Brown Sherbon, "Women in Medicine," *Medical Woman's Journal* 33 (September, 1925), 240-241 (hereafter cited as *MWJ*).

[35]Colwell, "Present Needs of Medical Education," 839.

[36]Burton D. Meyers, "Report on Applications for Matriculation in Schools of Medicine in the United States and Canada, 1929-1930," *AAMC Journal* 5 (March, 1930), 65-66, 83.

[37]Burton D. Meyers, "Report on Application for Matriculation in Schools of Medicine for 1927-1928," *AAMC Bulletin* 3 (July, 1928), 198.

[38]Zapffe, 233-234.

[39]Wilburt C. Davison, "Selection of Medical Students," *Southern Medical Journal* 20 (December, 1927), 955-957.

[40]Meyers, "Report on Applications, 1929-1930," 87-88.

[41]Ibid., 88.

[42]See "Medical Education Numbers," for 1920-1930.

[43]Bertha Van Hoosen, "Quo Vadis?" *MWJ* 36 (January, 1929), 2-3.

[44]"Report of the National Committee on Medical Opportunities for Women," *MWJ* 37 (July, 1930), 200.

[45]Curtis, 140-148.

[46]Van Hoosen, 2.

[47]Although women made up a smaller proportion of the graduates than of the students three years previous to the graduation date, it does not necessarily follow that women were leaving medical school at a greater rate than men. The statistics do not take into consideration the varying lengths of programs (some required a year of internship and others worked on a quarter system which allowed students to finish early). The "Medical Education Numbers" contained data on graduates.

[48]Carnegie Foundation for the Advancement of Teaching, *Seventeenth Annual Report* (1922), 86-88.

[49]Doerschuk, *Women in the Law,* 19.

[50]The figures were compiled from the "Biennial Survey of Education" for the years 1920-1930. Because the Bureau of Education relied on voluntary reporting, the statistics are incomplete. They are, however, the only figures for law schools that were tabulated according to sex. Most of the accredited schools sent in their enrollment figures, but part-time schools were more lax. Enrollment and graduate statistics are summarized in Tables 3 and 4 in the Appendix.

[51]BVI, *Training for the Professions and Allied Occupations,* 431.

[52]Auerbach, "Enmity and Amity," 572-580.

[53]Reed, *Training for the Public Profession of the Law,* 57-59, 399-401.

[54]Ibid., 398.

[55]Reed, *Training for the Public Profession of the Law,* 403-406, 414-419.

[56]Harlan J. Stone, "Legal Education and Democratic Principle," *ABAJ* 7 (December, 1921), 640.

[57]Stone did not alter his opinion with time. See Harlan J. Stone, "The Future of Legal Education," *ALSR* 5 (May, 1924), 329-334.

[58]Quoted in "Making the Law a Learned Profession," *Central Law Journal* 93 (September 23, 1921), 202.

[59]Alfred Z. Reed, "Raising the Standards of Legal Education," *ABAJ* 7 (November, 1921), 574.

[60]Carnegie Foundation for the Advancement of Teaching, *Sixteenth Annual Report* (1921), 86-88.

[61]"Menace of the Plutocratic Bar," *Journal of the American Judicature Society* 5 (February, 1922), 131; I. Maurice Wormser, "Problem of the Evening Law School," *ALSR* 4 (November, 1920), 544.

[62]Reed, *Training for the Public Profession of the Law,* 283.

[63]The *ABAJ* carried annual listings of approved schools after 1923.

[64]Carnegie Foundation for the Advancement of Teaching, *Nineteenth Annual Report* (1924), 69-70.

[65]Merton L. Ferson, "Law Aptitude Examinations," *ALSR* 5 (December, 1925), 563-565; Charles E. Clark, "The Law School and the Student: Admission and Exclusion of Students," *ALSR* 7 (April, 1932), 397-399.

[66]Alfred Z. Reed, *Present-Day Law Schools in the United States and Canada* (New York: D. B. Updike, 1928), 120.

[67]U. S., Department of the Interior, Bureau of Education, "Legal Education, 1925-1928," *Bulletin*, No. 31 (1929), 15.

[68]James R. Angell, "Economic Conditions and Educational Opportunities for Students to Obtain a Legal Education Requiring Two Years of College Training," *ABAJ* 8 (March, 1922), 144-145.

[69]"Self-Help for College Students," 75-134.

[70]Member schools of the AALS were used for 1920 and 1922, and the schools approved by the ABA Council on Legal Education were used after 1923. See Tables 3 and 4 in the Appendix.

[71]Doerschuk, 28.

[72]Ellen Spencer Mussey, "Women Attorneys," *ABAJ* 9 (January, 1923), 62-63; Marion Weston Cottle, "The Prejudice Against Women Lawyers: How Can it Be Overcome?" *Case and Comment* 21 (October, 1914), 372.

[73]In 1922, the *ALSR* began collecting enrollment data in October of each year. It had the most complete statistics for law schools during the twenties but they are nevertheless incomplete. Some of the schools missed the publication deadline each year, and the statistics did not take into account students who joined the course mid-year or who dropped out. In 1958, the American Bar Foundation published *Compilation of Published Statistics on Law School Enrollments and Admissions to the Bar, 1889-1957* (n.p.: American Bar Foundation, 1958). The over-all figures for attrition are from the latter document while those for individual schools came from the *ALSR* for the years 1923-1930.

[74]*The Law Student*, Vols. 1-7 (1923-1930) published bar examination statistics. They are incomplete but the best available.

[75]Ellahue Ansile Harper, "How to Raise the Standard of Morals for the Legal Profession," *Dickinson Law Review* 29 (January, 1925), 97.

[76]Harper, "How to Raise the Standard of Morals for the Legal Profession, 97; see *The Law Student*, 1923-1930, for statistics on bar exams failures.

[77]Quoted in "Higher Educational Standards Urged for Admission to Study Law in New York," *ALSR* 6 (May, 1927), 142-143.

[78]"Higher Educational Standards Urged for Admission to Study Law in New York," *ALSR* 6 (May, 1927), 142-143.

[79]I. Maurice Wormser, "Fewer Lawyers and Better Ones," 208; "Higher Educational Standards Urged for Admission to Study Law in New York," 142-143.

[80]"Biennial Survey of Education, 1928-1930," *Bulletin*, No. 20 (1931), 338-339.

[81]Lindsey R. Harmon and Herbert Soldz, *Doctorate Production in the United States Universities, 1920-1962* (Washington, D.C.: National Academy of Science and National Research Council, 1963), 50-51.

[82]Quoted in *AAUP Bulletin* 7 (January-February, 1921), 17.

[83]"Educational Research and Statistics," *School and Society* 12 (October 30, 1920), 412-413; "How Professors Live," *School and Society* 12 (November 6, 1920), 437-439.

[84]Frederick A. Ogg, *Research in the Humanities and Social Sciences* (New York: Century Company, 1928), 16, 157, 281-822; Slosson, *The Great Crusade and After,* 332.

[85]In his annual address to the AAUP, President Arthur O. Lovejoy marked the beginning of professional identity for college teachers with the founding of the AAUP in 1915. See Lovejoy, 10.

[86]Many college officials complained that the prerequisites of professional schools, such as medicine, and graduate schools not only turned liberal arts colleges into vocational schools but also forced institutions to adhere to standards not of their own making. See Leon B. Richardson, "The Liberal College and Vocationalism," *AAU Proceedings* 27 (1925), 44-46.

[87]Harmon and Soldz, 1.

[88]Harmon and Soldz, 42-43; "Scholarships and Fellowships," 68-115.

[89]The average time-lapse for chemistry was 6.2 years and for engineering, 6.9 years during the twenties. Harmon and Soldz, 42-43.

[90]In its biennial surveys of education, the Bureau of Education gave the enrollment statistics and number of Ph.D.'s by institution and sex. It was the only organization to do so.

[91]"Biennial Survey of Education, 1928-1930," 338-339; "Scholarships and Fellowships," 68-115.

[92]"Scholarships and Fellowships," 68-115.

[93]Emilie J. Hutchinson, "Women and the Ph.D.," *Journal of the American Association of University Women* 22 (October, 1928), 20 (hereafter cited as *AAUW Journal*).

[94]Harmon and Soldz, 42-43.

[95]"Scholarships and Fellowships," 68-115.

[96]N. B. Davis to Emma P. Hirth, August 27, 1921, BVI Papers, Box 22, Scientific Work: Chemistry in Industry.

[97]Hugh K. Moore to Emma P. Hirth, October, 1921, BVI Papers, Box 23, Scientific Work: Chemistry in Industry.

[98]"Scholarships and Fellowships," 74-76.

[99]"Biennial Survey of Education, 1928-1930," 338; Harmon and Soldz, 50-51.

[100]"Faculty Training in Liberal Arts Colleges," *North Central Association Quarterly* 3 (September, 1928), 173-175.

[101]Martha Tracy, "Profession of Medicine and Women's Opportunities," *AAUW Journal* 21 (October, 1927), 5.

[102]Dr. Rosalie Slaughter Morton, a noted surgeon, said that only those women training for missionary careers should attempt going through medical school without income or strong financial support. Rosalie Slaughter Morton, *A Woman Surgeon* (New York: Frederick A. Stokes, 1937), 23.

[103]"Medical Education Numbers," 1920-1930.

CHAPTER IV

WOMEN PRACTITIONERS IN THE 1920's

During the 1920's, 1,881 women graduated from medical colleges, 1,816 women earned doctorates, and over 3,500 women graduated from law schools.[1] Despite the unquestionable importance of educational background in influencing the direction and scope of an individual's career, possession of a degree did not guarantee the holder a position or future success. It was as practitioners, not as students, that their colleagues and society judged professional women. As practitioners women also encountered the full force of traditional prejudice and institutional obstacles which limited their achievements. Talent, personal sacrifice, and strength of mind, body, and character were necessary attributes for the women who would succeed in the male-dominated professions of medicine, law, and college teaching.

Evaluating the success of a person or group may be done in many different ways. The laity, lacking the technical knowledge of the professions, has tended to rely on superficial, visible criteria: income, social prestige, and fame. More important to the female participants themselves was the recognition of those who did actually understand their work—professional colleagues who awarded prizes, appointments, and offices and who listened to papers and read publications. On yet another level was the individual's perception of her own worth, whether or not she thought her work was important and satisfied her personal goals. Women professionals tended to be reticent about their accomplishments, and their male colleagues often minimized or ignored what women were doing. Concrete data on female practitioners are sketchy at best and, consequently, suggestive rather than conclusive.

All the evidence indicates that if a woman managed to go through her professional training unscathed and undaunted by masculine prejudice, she was virtually certain to meet it head on upon graduation. In medicine, this occurred when women tried to find internships and residencies. Established women doctors urged their neophyte sisters to get the same advanced training as men, advice that was easier to give than to follow. The seeming availability of positions for women interns was misleading. Dr. Bertha Van Hoosen, a noted surgeon, obstetrician, and junior editor of the *Medical Woman's Journal (MWJ)*, made a detailed survey of opportunities for women interns in 1926. She found that 127 hospitals, with a total of 1,047 internships, reported they accepted women, more than enough for all the female graduates that year. "When actually put to the test," cautioned Dr. Van Hoosen, "many of these hospitals will not consider a woman intern unless it is impossible to get a desirable man."[2]   Pennsylvania, New York, California, and Illinois abounded with opportunities for women, but seventeen states had no hospitals whatever which accepted female interns.   Administrators most often cited the difficulty of arranging living quarters for women doctors, a specious argument in cases where hospitals housed women nurses.   Rhode Island Hospital in Providence, for example, used that excuse for rejecting female interns but qualified its rules by adding: "Pathological service may be an exception."[3]   Administrators could change their policies when it suited their needs.

Some hospitals, however, refused prospective women interns because of unfavorable past experiences.   Nearly a third of the hospitals responded that female interns were not as good as male interns.   Women sometimes were unwilling to take shifts on the ambulance or genito-urinary services, and some hospitals were reluctant to assign women to the latter.[4]   Dr. Van Hoosen berated the younger generation: "This is no time for medical women to dare lag behind or look for special favors."[5]   She urged them to revive the pioneer spirit that had characterized her own generation.

The difficulties of securing an internship were magnified if a woman wanted post-graduate training in a specialized field.   The justifications against women residents and interns were similar except in the case of the former there was the additional contention that it was wasteful to train women because they invariably married or dropped out of practice.   Some doctors guessed the attrition rate of women from the profession at 50 percent.[6]   Marriage, however, did not prevent women from using their medical training.   Both the 1920 and 1930 censuses showed that a third of the female doctors were married.[7]   Dr. Martha Tracy, in her study of women who graduated from medical school between 1905 and 1910 and between 1912 and 1921, found that, of those who had married, only 13.9 percent of the first group and 12.8 percent of the second group had ceased practice entirely.   Furthermore, she discovered that only 9.1 percent of all women doctors in her survey had dropped out of medicine.[8]   Two Barnard professors, Florence Lowther and Helen Downes, found that 90 percent of those women who graduated from seven eastern medical schools between 1921 and 1940 had full-time medical careers in 1945, and of those who had married, 82 percent had remained in full-time practice.[9]   In spite of this record, the myth of the high attrition rate persisted throughout the twenties adding to the impediments women doctors faced.[10]

Internships and residencies served important functions besides adding to the experience and self-confidence of the young doctor: they could also advance a career.   Since the ethics of the medical profession forbade self-advertisement, doctors relied heavily on referrals for building practices. Professional contacts could also ease the way to appointments on hospital staffs, in institutions, and in medical faculties. Women physicians needed these contacts as much as their colleagues did, if not more so.

Most medical school graduates did go through a year of internship before starting practice.[11] In other respects as well, women's careers paralleled men's. The vast majority of physicians went into private practice rather than educational, research, or institutional work. Women and men showed a tendency to specialize after a few years of general practice. Doctors of both sexes concentrated most heavily in New York, Pennsylvania, Massachusetts, Ohio, Illinois, and California and least heavily in the states of the Great Plains. The exception was the South where a disproportionately small number of females practiced. It was also true that women followed the general trend of concentrating in urban areas.[13] However, dissimilarities between male and female practitioners also existed.

After a few years of general practice characterized by long hours, low recompense, and the struggle to keep abreast of many different fields, many women specialized. In 1927, Dr. Tracy found that of the women who graduated between 1905 and 1910, 39.5 percent combined general practice with some specialty work and 37.7 percent engaged wholly in specialties. Of the women graduates for the years 1912 to 1921, 30.5 percent combined general and specialty work while 50 percent were full-time specialists.[13] In comparison, Dr. H. G. Weiskotten, who surveyed the classes of 1915 and 1920, found that 23.2 percent of the graduates were in general practice, 37.9 in specialties, and 38 percent combined the two.[14] Male and female physicians varied in their concentration within the specialties. Weiskotten found the most popular fields for men were eye, ear, nose and throat; internal medicine; surgery; and pediatrics.[15] Dr. Tracy found women specialized most often in gynecology and obstetrics; internal medicine; ear, nose, and throat; and pathology.[16]

The areas in which women concentrated reflected their interests and the fields most open to feminine intrusion. Many people, both within and without the profession, thought that women were peculiarly fitted for the fields of pediatrics and obstetrics.[17] Since time immemorial women had cared for the health of their children and presided over births, hence the two specialties were regarded as natural extensions of the feminine role. Although some women doctors scoffed at being relegated to "women's jobs," Dr. S. Josephine Baker, director of the Bureau of Child Hygiene in New York City, the first of its kind in the world, pointed out that they were "godsends" for the young doctor:

It is one of the sure events in medicine, for babies are always with us. It is an opening wedge of considerable importance to have an obstetric case, stay on as the baby's doctor and then, when in the natural order of events the father or mother comes down with a cold or some other minor ailment, to find that you are consulted and have other patients.[18]

In addition, the two fields did not absolutely require hospital affiliation: most childhood diseases and obstetric cases were treated in the home in the twenties.[19] The nature of the work involved long hours, night work, low fees, and house calls. Nevertheless, because of the strong social precedents, women practitioners found the resistance to their entry into pediatrics and obstetrics less than in other fields.

By contrast, female doctors found it difficult to specialize in some of the more prestigious fields such as surgery. The introduction of antiseptics, anesthesia, and x-ray in the preceding fifty years had dramatically increased the safety and success of operations and augmented the eminence of surgeons. But gaining this position entailed a three-year, post-graduate training program and hospital affiliation. In 1926, there were fifty-one women Fellows of the American College of Surgeons, the body representing the elite of the surgical world. Thirty-three of the women had either attended a women's medical college or trained in a woman's hospital. Furthermore, twenty-four of the doctors had graduated from medical school prior to 1900, twenty between 1900 and 1915, but only one since 1915.[20] Because of the reduced number of women's medical schools, the failure of some women's hospitals to qualify as training centers for residencies, and the reluctance of other hospitals to train females, opportunities for women to become surgeons appeared to be diminishing.

Even more serious for women surgeons and other specialists was the difficulty of securing staff appointments in hospitals. The borough of Manhattan, with between three and four hundred women physicians as against over five thousand male physicians, was typical.[21] In thirteen general hospitals in the city in 1929, women doctors filled only eleven out of a total of 1,072 staff positions. In the six largest non-municipal hospitals in the city, women filled only six positions out of 528. Most of the women served as assistants, and only one was an attending physician on a surgical staff. Only the New York Infirmary for Women and Children, founded Drs. Elizabeth and Emily Blackwell to give women doctors a chance to practice their profession, and Booth Memorial Hospital had female chiefs of staff.[22] At the time, a proposed merger of the New York Infirmary with Columbia University Hospital threatened to reduce further women's opportunities: after the merger, only 3 to 5 percent of the staff positions would be filled by women, and even those were not guaranteed.[23] The discriminatory behavior of hospitals hurt not only the women practitioners but also their patients since the doctors were denied the use of essential equipment and facilities.

The limited access to hospital privileges helped to explain why women physicians rarely contributed to the art and science of medicine. The development of new surgical techniques, for example, occurred most often in a hospital environment. But it was equally true that few women joined the staffs of either institutes or medical faculties where the bulk of the research was done. Dr. Van Hoosen found that approximately 7.5 percent of all female doctors were engaged in research on either a part-time or a full-time basis.[24] Individuals like Alice Hamilton, Assistant Professor Industrial Medicine at Harvard, and Florence Sabin, Professor of Histology at Johns Hopkins and later a researcher at the Rockefeller Institute, earned world-wide reputations, but they were part of a tiny minority. If publications in medical journals were any indication, it appeared that male colleagues lacked confidence in women's abilities as researchers. "The larger medical journals are willing to publish a limited number of good papers written by women," commented an editorial.[25] But in 1926 five-eighths of all medical articles written by women doctors appeared in the *MWJ.*[26]

As in other branches of medicine, the top ranks of teaching were beyond the reach of women. A total of 198 medical women taught at forty-three Class A schools in 1927, but most of them were instructors. Women attained the rank of full professor at only six schools, and only at Loyola University Medical School and Women's Medical College did they head departments.[27] The women who succeeded were uncommonly good and often unique. Dr. Alice Hamilton became the first woman on the Harvard faculty because the school could find no one else to teach industrial medicine, a field she had pioneered.[28] Similarly, the administrators of New York University-Bellevue Hospital School bowed to the request of Dr. Josephine Baker that she be admitted as the first female degree candidate in their new program in public health in exchange for teaching a course on child hygiene, her specialty.[29]

Despite their best efforts, women often met with slights and rebuffs in medical faculties. Dr. Hamilton had an international reputation through her frequent publications and papers and through her work on the Health Committee on the League of Nations, yet Harvard never promoted her above the rank of assistant professor.[30] The AMA Council on Medical Education advised Loyola to remove Dr. Van Hoosen as head of the department of obstetrics because she was a woman. Loyola did not follow the advice.[31] Dr. Sabin left Johns Hopkins partly because she was passed over as the successor to Dr. Franklin Mall's professorship in microbiology, even though she was the logical choice. When her students protested, the administrators appointed her to the professorship of histology as a consolation.[32] If women were not achieving the top ranks in medical faculties, the prejudice of male administrators and faculty members rather than any defect in women's abilities was at least partly responsible.

Medical women appeared to be making gains in salaried positions, however. In several instances, new legislation opened opportunities for women. Many states had laws requiring the employment of female physicians in penal institutions, asylums, and sanitaria for women. In marked contrast, states without such legislation employed very few women doctors.[33] The passage of the Sheppard-Towner Bill in 1922 helped establish or enlarge bureaus of child hygiene in most states. All but three of the forty-one bureaus were headed by women, of whom twenty-four were physicians. Women doctors participated heavily on the local level as well.[34] In addition, public health programs, girls' schools, and industries and businesses employing large numbers of working girls found it expedient to use women doctors. There were, of course, drawbacks to salaried work. Much of it involved administration, inspections, and routine check-ups rather than actual patient care. Working for a government could mean entanglement in bureaucratic red tape and uncertainty about funds and support. The work often lacked prestige, and the pay, even if steadier than the fees of the private practitioner, was low. In 1920, schools generally paid about $1,800 plus maintenance; state institutions, between $1,600 and $2,000 plus maintenance; and social agencies, a starting salary of $1,800 to $2,000.[35]

Although women in private practice usually earned more than their sisters in salaried positions, women in general earned less than their male colleagues did. The median annual income for all physicians during the twenties was $4,600, and for all doctors graduated from Class A schools after 1918, it was $6,070.[36] In contrast, a survey of the members of the Business and Professional Women's Clubs showed that the women with medical degrees had a median income of $2,932.[37] Whereas an estimated 11.5 percent of all doctors earned over $11,000 in 1929, Dr. Tracy found that only 4 percent of her sample earned over $10,000.[38] The discrepancy between men's and women's earnings reflected the prevailing trend of paying women less than men, women's concentration in less remunerative fields and neighborhoods, and philanthropic work.

Income was not the sole measure of achievement; equally important was the approval of the profession. One woman doctor voiced the opinion that the men had little use for female doctors as a class but liked individuals well enough.[39] Indeed Florence Sabin, Alice Hamilton, and Josephine Baker received honor and acclaim from the profession and the public. More typically, however, women doctors played a negligible role in the profession itself. Although the AMA admitted female members in 1915, during the next fifteen years only one woman was elected to the office of vice-president and a scattering served as Delegates.[40] Of the 327 papers presented at the AMA Convention in 1921, two had women authors and four had women co-authors. At the 1924 meeting, eleven women presented papers.[41]

Women fared little better in state, local, or specialty societies than they did in the AMA. Although an occasional woman presided over a society, most of the female officers served as secretaries or treasurers. Their participation in meetings was not remarkable either. An examination of programs from fifty state societies in 1928 revealed that seventeen of them had no female participants.[42] Admittedly, women showed some reluctance to present or discuss papers, but neither did the societies encourage them to do so. Local societies, most notably in the South, and some specialty societies, particularly gynecological and surgical, still refused to admit female members.[43] Even when nominally admitted, women doctors were sometimes barred from formal and informal meetings which were often held in men's clubs.[44] Women had practiced medicine over seventy years by the twenties, but they were still treated as outsiders.

As a group, women physicians received negligible recognition from the medical brotherhood because they were most effective and interested in fields which were deemed relatively unimportant or even contrary to the interests of the profession. The ideal of the scientist-doctor dominated medicine during the twenties, and those who discovered cures or illuminated the mysterious workings of the body won the acclaim.[45] Women doctors, however, more often devoted their energies to preventive medicine and humanitarian activities. The far-flung series of American Women's Hospitals, founded during World War I because the United States Army refused the service of women surgeons, continued relief work after the Armistice. By the end of the decade, the organization established and ran seventy-two hospitals in France, Serbia, Turkey, Russia, Armenia, and Japan. The governments of these countries bestowed honors and thanks on the women, but almost the only medical journal in the United States to mention their work was the *Medical Woman's Journal*.[46] Likewise, the work of women medical missionaries in India and China, where females were more effective than males in reaching the natives through their treatment of women and children, went almost entirely unnoticed by the profession.[47]

On the home front, vocal members of the medical sisterhood, represented by the members of the Medical Women's National

Association, sometimes championed causes which put them at odds with the rest of the profession. Concerned about infringements on the practice of medicine by state or national governments, the AMA condemned anything that remotely resembled state medicine, whether it was the Volstead Act or the Sheppard-Towner Act.[48] Women physicians supported both, but particularly the latter.[49] Always interested in preventive medicine and the care of their sex and of children, women applauded the Sheppard-Towner Act because it sought to reduce the risks of maternity and infancy by providing pre- and post-natal care at government expense. It brought into contact with physicians and nurses underprivileged women who otherwise would have consulted untrained midwives or no one at all. Opponents, invoking state's rights and professional autonomy, often missed the point of the act. One critical pamphlet branded it as "'paternalism, communism, sovietism, and all the isms condensed into one,'" and deprecated it because half the advisory committees in each state would be composed of women.[50] For the AMA, the sanctity of professional autonomy seemingly outweighed the well-being of women and children. With leading women doctors, it appeared to be just the opposite.[51]

Clearly, medical women fulfilled their professional obligations and did so in the face of major obstacles. Despite restrictions on advanced training, hospital affiliation, and membership in medical societies, women practiced their calling and worked to improve the health of the nation. If few women reached the top ranks, it was because of the barriers in their paths and because their accomplishments went unrecognized by the profession.

For female lawyers, the difficulties of medical women were not only present but magnified as the available statistics clearly indicated. The 1920 census reported 1,738 female attorneys in the United States; during the following decade, over 3,500 women graduated from law schools and an unknown number studied in schools or read law in private offices before taking bar exams. Yet, by 1930, the number of women lawyers had grown by only 1,643. It was true that male graduates also did not practice law, but their attrition rate from the profession was not as high as women's.[52] Evidently, many of those who studied law never practiced it or were transient members of the profession. The law was good preparation for careers in business or politics. The conditions within the profession with which women attorneys grappled, however, helped to explain their poor representation.

Although some states had admitted women to the bar as early as the 1870's, the woman lawyer was still a relative newcomer in the twenties. California, Illinois, Massachusetts, and New York each had over a hundred women attorneys in 1920, but eight states had fewer than five and twenty-one states had fewer than fifteen.[53] In areas where few women had practiced, particularly in the South, female attorneys became local curiosities, asked to speak at clubs or give the "feminine view" of an issue but not legal opinions.[54] One woman lawyer, Margaret J. Carns, thought that, because women had been classified with chattels for so many generations, attorneys and laymen had not yet adapted to the new feminine status.[55]

Being a female created a problem of identity for women lawyers: they continually fought against a negative stereotype. Unlike medicine, there were few social precedents for women acting as attorneys in behalf of others, and those forerunners were buried in history. Certain aspects of the profession were thought to be incongruous with feminine character. In corporate law, for example, the current practice in at least some quarters was to "do your neighbor and do him first," a philosophy that Sophonisba Breckinridge thought most women could not accept.[56] Taboos surrounded trial work. Even female lawyers themselves sometimes conceded to these constraints. As one woman put it:

> To my mind, it's unbecoming for a woman to be engaged even in a legal battle, and participation in it belittles her in the esteem of others, whereas it would be an asset to a man. When a woman loses her femininity in the pursuit of her profession, she has lost much more than she can possibly hope to gain.[57]

Whether or not women became mannish through the practice of law, they reassured themselves and the public at every opportunity that a good lawyer could also be feminine. After meeting Grace Hays Riley, Dean of the Washington College of Law, Maryland attorney Henrietta Dunlop Stonestreet remarked that

> It was indeed encouraging to those of us who had decided to follow the actual practice of the law to realize that a woman might be as successful as Dean Riley has been, and yet retain such a charming personality, . . .[58]

Nonetheless, the prevalent view of their unsuitability for the rough and tumble of the law appears to have kept many women from practicing.

The women lawyers who did establish independent practices found their sex a handicap in other ways as well. Most clients were male, and there was no "natural" female or child clientele. In fact, Judge Jean H. Norris warned, "Probably the worst prejudice that women lawyers ever encountered, . . . arose from members of their own sex."[59] As lawyers, some women discovered that they served in a peculiar capacity. "Too often they are regarded as philanthropic advisors, . . . like the religious confessor who bears the burden of other folks' troubles without fees or reward on earth," complained an editorial in the *Women Lawyers' Journal*.[60] Indeed, the difficulty of finding paying clients meant that it frequently took a woman lawyer five years to become self-supporting.[61] Nor was it easy for her to find financial backing for those early years. An attorney wrote:

> A father, older brother or sister will eagerly fit out and support a young man lawyer, believing he will succeed eventually. But a young woman, they cannot recall a woman who made good in the neighborhood and do not encourage her venturing alone.[62]

Most practitioners could not afford an extensive law library of their own, so they relied on that of the county society. Women found that many county bar societies were still closed to their sex in the twenties, thus inhibiting their use of this valuable resource.[63] For the individual woman, hanging out a shingle sounded easier than it proved to be in practice.

Since starting one's own practice was filled with hazards, the logical alternative was to go into partnership or join an established firm. Most firms, however, did not want women lawyers. Mrs. Alice Boarman Baldridge's case was typical. A widow with three years of experience in another state, she decided to practice law in New York City. Despite good recommendations and influential friends, it took her months to find a position. The women's firms had no vacancies, and the men were not interested in her unless she would double as a secretary or stenographer, something not required of male clerks.[64] Other women attorneys faced the same problem. Although many clerical workers took law courses to improve their salaries as secretaries or possibly in hopes of eventually becoming a partner in the office, all the advice literature cautioned women against this path. Judge Norris warned future lawyers:

> But never, under any circumstances, unless actual bread and butter—and by this the writer does not mean even simple luxuries—actually depend on it, take a position as a stenographer in a law office. This has proved fatal to too many promising young women. . . . A young woman lawyer who is also a stenographer will be considered by the office staff in terms of a stenographer and not in terms of a lawyer.[65]

In truth, women lawyers were of limited value to most law firms. Few women became trial lawyers because of the stigma attached to the work, and they lacked the necessary connections to succeed as corporate lawyers. As latecomers to the political world, women were not in a position to make or receive political promises.[66] Clients of either sex were reluctant to confide in female attorneys or trust their judgment, and the usual paths of communication within the profession—informal meetings and memberships in local associations—were more often than not closed to them. Their value to an office rested on their ability to do the toilsome background work. Dean H. S. Richards of the law school of the University of Wisconsin put the problem succinctly:

> I do not know any women in the state who have attained any reputation at the bar. Their work is apt to be in the office side, which is the inconspicuous side, and therefore does not so readily come to the attention of the public or the authorities.[67]

Women were perpetual subordinates in most law firms, rarely rising in the office hierarchy.

Since it was so difficult for women either to establish private practices or to find suitable positions in other firms, is it not surprising to find that they often chanelled their training and energies in other directions outside the profession. At the same time, it was true that many women took law courses with the object of improving their salaries as secretaries or getting better jobs in business. In her survey of job opportunities for Southern women in 1926, Dr. Orie Latham Hatcher found that women attorneys held a wide variety of positions. Of the nine female attorneys in Richmond, Virginia, two were secretaries in law offices, one worked in an insurance company, and another was compiling a digest of laws for social workers. In Atlanta, Georgia, the positions held by eleven women lawyers included those of stenographer, realtor, cashier in a loan company, clerk in a trust company, reporter, and assistant district attorney.[68] Women with legal training were far from idle even if they generally worked in positions below their level of training.

In spite of all the plausible reasons for quitting or finding some other line of employment, more than three thousand women decided to practice law, either independently or as members of firms. An evaluation of their sucess, as in the case of medical women, was hampered by their own reticence and that of their professional colleagues. Certainly women earned considerably less than their male colleagues did. The median annual income for all lawyers during the twenties was $4,000.[69] Beatrice Doerschuk found, however, that the women lawyers in her survey in the early years of the decade earned a median yearly income of $2,000.[70] The survey of the members of the Business and Professional Women's Clubs revealed that women with law degrees had median earnings of $2,346.[71] The amount a woman attorney earned naturally depended on the length of her experience, the kind of practice or position she had, and her location. Income was not, however, a reliable measure of success.

As in the case of medical women, female attorneys longed for recognition from their male colleagues. But because the law was a highly conservative profession, women lawyers fought an uphill battle. Lawyer Grace Rohleder observed, in the mid-twenties, that male attorneys held a proprietary attitude about the law:

> They hold the delusion that the law is their field and that woman's venture into the profession is an intrusion—a trespass upon their rights. . . . The woman lawyer has occupied an undesirably isolated position which has been a great disadvantage, and the women who have come to the front deserve more credit.[72]

At best, the men of the profession treated women lawyers with a misplaced chivalry. The ABA, which admitted female members on the same basis as males in 1918, also appointed women to positions on committees. The committees, however, were usually the least important ones, such as the Committee on Memorials. When the president and vice-president of the National Association of Women Lawyers reported for their first meeting of the Reception Committee, they found that their appointment carried no duties.[73] Significantly, women did not appear on the convention programs of the ABA, and few articles by women appeared in law journals other than the *Women Lawyers' Journal.* As in the case of medical women, this may have reflected reluctance on the part of women lawyers to present papers or write articles as much as reluctance on the part of associations or journals to have female participants.[74] On the local level, women belonged to and occasionally served as officers of state and county societies, but only the Women Lawyers Associations sent female representatives to special meetings of the profession.[75] Although the men behaved graciously to women lawyers admitted to their ranks, for the most part, they remained unconvinced that women had anything worthwhile to contribute to the profession.

Not all the men of the legal brotherhood held female attorneys in low esteem. After all, men made the appointments to judgeships, commissions, and positions such as assistant district attorney, all of which women held during the twenties. It was common, however, for women to be relegated to certain kinds of work. Robert C. Crowe, State's Attorney for Illinois, decided to appoint one or more women assistants in Cook County specifically to deal with female defendants:

The average woman is more competent to understand the problems of a delinquent girl or woman and for this reason I think both the state and the defendant will be more sure of receiving justice with a woman prosecutor.[76]

Likewise, women appeared on the bench first in juvenile and family courts and in other courts of limited jurisdiction. Although women judges of the twenties won recognition primarily as pathbreakers for their sex, it was significant that several aquitted themselves well enough to merit reappointment, re-election, or advancement in the judicial hierarchy. In the District of Columbia, Katherine Sellers, Judge of the Juvenile Court, and Mary O'Toole, Judge of the Municipal Court, served multiple terms. Florence Allen was initially appointed to an unexpired term on the municipal bench in Cleveland, Ohio, but she won reelection to the position and eventually was elected to the Supreme Court of Ohio. Similarly, Mary Bartelme began as Judge of the Juvenile Courts in Chicago but won election to the Supreme Court of Illinois.[77] Characteristically, these women carried out their duties without fanfare as it behooved members of their profession.

Women attorneys made little impact on their field largely because they were seldom trial or corporate lawyers, United States Supreme Court Justices, or law school professors who stood out in the profession. Furthermore, even when women lawyers did speak out, they usually confined themselves to issues concerning women and children. A faction of the legal sorority, by no means unopposed, felt strongly that women attorneys should bend their efforts to improving legislation for their sex and children. Consequently, the *Women Lawyers' Journal* carried on discussions about uniform marriage and divorce laws, legislation concerning the rights and duties of married women, the Child Labor Amendment, and the Equal Rights Amendment. Women lawyers kept abreast of developments in their own states, petitioned legislatures, spoke to women's clubs, and worked to defeat unfavorable bills.[78] But while the rest of the profession thought in terms of torts and contracts, criminal, corporate, tax, and international law, women tended to identify themselves far more narrowly. As in the case of female doctors, much of the work of women laywers went unnoticed.

Women in higher education, unlike their sisters in medicine and law, did not encounter a firm wall of resistance in the 1920's. With the rapid expansion of college enrollment, women teachers more than doubled their numbers during the decade and increased their relative strength in the profession from 30.1 to 32 percent. Always prominent in women's colleges, academic women appeared to be gaining ground elsewhere as well. In 1921, the preliminary report of Committee W on the Status of Women in Colleges and Universities of the AAUP stated that many coeducational colleges were reconsidering their negative views on women teachers. In fact, twelve such schools had appointed their first female teachers in the preceding two years. Alone among men's institutions, Harvard and Yale had also hired their first women at the graduate level.[79] As members of the academic profession, women participated actively in the AAUP and other professional societies. Yet the picture was not one of unalloyed optimism. The very existence of Committee W indicated that women, while not a negligible group in the profession, had not achieved the recognition they felt they deserved.

The preliminary report of committee W, which surveyed fourteen major women's colleges and a hundred coeducational institutions with a combined teaching staff of 13,858, illustrated just how far women still had to go to achieve equality with men in the profession. Women comprised 75 percent of the teaching staffs of women's colleges but only 12.8 percent of those in coeducational schools where 31 percent of the student population was female. In both kinds of schools, females concentrated most heavily in the lower ranks. They made up 23.5 percent of the instructors but only 7.9 percent of all professors in coeducational colleges. To a certain extent, this concentration may have reflected women's relatively recent entry into coeducational institutions. In women's colleges, females made up 86 percent of the professors and 67.7 percent of the instructors. Significantly, more than half of the male teachers at women's colleges were full professors and they represented 45 percent of all faculty members of that rank. In coed schools, however, only 11.5 percent of all women teachers achieved the highest rank, and they made up only 4 percent of all full professors.[80]

Academic women tended to concentrate in certain fields that reflected their interests and their opportunities for advancement. Aside from the obvious "female subjects" of home economics and women's physical education, women were most likely to be found in humanities, social sciences, and education and least likely in the natural sciences. Although women could achieve top ranks in any field at a women's college, this was not generally true at a coeducational institution. Committee W discovered that, with the elimination of home economics and physical education, less than 3 percent of the full professorships at coeducational schools were held by women.[81]

Rank and the institution where a person taught were the two major determinants of a teacher's salary. The size, location, and type of school affected what a teacher could earn. Because of the relatively small endowments, women's colleges generally paid less than either men's or coeducational schools did. Compare, for example, the average salaries for all professors at three different sizes of schools for 1926-1927.[82]

Men's & Coed Schools	Class A	Class B	Class C
Professor	$4,620	$3,355	$2,726
Associate Professor	3,547	2,741	2,435
Assistant Professor	2,833	2,461	2,169
Instructor	2,000	1,890	1,623

Women's Schools			
Professor	4,049	3.244	2,860
Associate Professor	3,299	2,488	2,509
Assistant Professor	2,666	2,283	2,058
Instructor	1,977	1,881	1,684

Since most females taught at women's colleges and settled in the lower ranks, as a group, they earned less than their male colleagues earned for comparable work.

The wide disparity of pay scales for different schools presented only a general picture; more informative were the policies of individual institutions toward faculty men and women. The report of Committee W revealed that 47 percent of coeducational schools and 27 percent of the women's colleges admitted frankly that women were given both lower rank and pay for doing the same work as their male coworkers. The variance between men's and women's salaries ranged from 10 to 50 percent and averaged 18 percent. In schools where the pay scale was the same for both sexes, women advanced more slowly than men did.[83] Administrators justified the discrepancy by citing the operation of supply and demand, men's need to support their families, and the social desirability of attracting men into the profession—arguments that might well have been applied equally to both sexes but were not.[84]

To a certain extent, women themselves could improve their rank and salary by earning a Ph.D. or publishing scholarly works. But like most young college teachers, they found themselves in the typical academic dilemma. Women concentrated in the lowest ranks where heavy teaching loads reduced available research time to a minimum during the school year. Low salaries sometimes did not cover the cost of research trips or equipment and forced young teachers to find second jobs to supplement their incomes. For those teaching in women's colleges or small co-educational schools, low endowments meant poor library and laboratory facilities and few grants for research. The levels above instructor paid better and had lighter teaching loads, but climbing to those ranks involved scholarly production. The system could weed out the mediocre, but it could also be a vicious circle.[85]

The academic system placed an additional handicap on its female members. At coeducational schools, and even at some women's colleges, men filled the majority of the chairmanships, deanships, and presidencies. The occupants of those positions, collectively or individually, decided the academic future of women teachers. Under the circumstances, two opinion surveys in the middle twenties on the performance of academic women were very revealing. One was the Second Report of Committee W on the Status of Women on College and University Faculties of the AAUP, which received answers from 109 men and forty-three women from eighty coeducational and thirteen women's colleges. The other survey, made by Ella Lonn for the American Association of University Women, sent questionnaires to the heads of the English, modern language, and social science departments at seventy coeducational universities.[86]   The opinions returned for the two surveys showed a noticeable coincidence despite differences in questions.

In both surveys, the majority of the respondents said that women equalled men as teachers and were conscientious in their duties and in keeping up with their fields. There was general agreement that faculty women were conversant with civic and university affairs and that they participated actively in both. The concensus was that women received the same treatment as men in regard to committee assignments, opportunities for research, course loads, and advanced classes. At the same time, however, respondents thought that men surpassed women in stimulating their students, particularly in advanced classes. In coeducational schools, women faced an additional handicap because male students showed a preference for men teachers. Finally the respondents thought men exceeded women in the production of scholarly works.[87]

The surveys would lead one to think that women received commensurate treatment with men and encountered minor obstacles, but despite this fact they did not fulfill their professional obligations. In fact the AAUW survey suggested:

> We need a larger supply of women adequately trained for advanced work. I know that many of my women coworkers are impatient of the complaint of a dearth of trained women, but I feel we cannot neglect the statement of so many fair-minded heads of departments.[88]

The advice was sage, but given some of the other information in the reports, it is questionable how much good the doctorate would have done. Both surveys were opinion polls that made no attempt to eliminate prejudice. In the AAUP report, where the responses were divided according to the sex of the replier, critical comments came far more frequently from males than from females.[89] Since most department chairmen and deans were men in the AAUW report, a negative conception of women's abilities among a sizeable proportion of the respondents was significant. The AAUW survey asked if promotion applied equally to men and women, and 92 percent of the answers were affirmative. Further inquiry elicited the information that 68.9 percent of the respondents would give preference to a man over an equally qualified woman and 36.4 percent would give preference to a male candidate even if the woman had superior qualifications and personality. Slightly more than half of the replies indicated that male academicians would prefer not to have women on the faculty.[90] The comments quoted below were typical:

> The majority of the men are not averse theoretically to a limited number of women in the *lower* positions and in the deanship, of course.

> They do not desire women except in departments other than their own and in positions lower than professors.

> A few women may contribute something useful to a university staff.[91]

Women in academia perceived their status from a different perspective and had a different evaluation of their opportunities for advancement. A study of female doctorates, appearing in 1928, seemed to contradict some of the statements of the earlier surveys. Of the approximately five hundred women in college teaching in the survey, 75 percent said they had found some opportunity to do research. But since only ninety women said they had held post-doctoral fellowships and fewer than a hundred reported having any leave of absence for research, it would appear that the opportunities were of their own making. The demands of an academic position presented the major obstacle to scholarly activity. Nevertheless, of those who found the time to do research, 53 percent had published scholarly works, primarily articles in scientific journals. That would mean that 39.6 percent of the college teachers in the survey had published.[92] Considering that most journals were run by men who might have demanded a higher standard of work from women than from men, it was not a contemptible record.

Despite the obstacle of traditional prejudice which handicapped women's progress in college teaching, female teachers fared better than their sisters in law or medicine. The existence of a few strong women's colleges where they were relatively free from the jealousies and competitions of male academicians enabled women to rise to the top of the teaching hierarchy and of their own disciplines. Perhaps because of this condition, men were willing to accept them in professional organizations. Women teachers were active in professional societies: the AAUW survey reported that 80 percent of the respondents belonged to at least one such organization.[93] Women were charter members of the AAUP in 1915, and throughout the twenties, three served as committee heads, eight were members of the Council, and two were vice-presidents.[94] In individual disciplines women also made an impact, though there was considerable variation from field to field. For example, within the social sciences, women wrote less than 3 percent of the articles appearing in either the *Quarterly Journal of Economics* or the *Political Science Quarterly* during the twenties. In contrast, they wrote nearly 15 percent of those in the *Journal of Applied Sociology* and in the *American Journal of Psychology* and 29 percent of those in the *Journal of Social Forces.*[95] Margaret Floy Washburn, Professor of Psychology and head of a unique experimental laboratory at Vassar, was so highly regarded in the field that a special commemorative volume of the *American Journal of Psychology*, which she had helped edit for many years, was dedicated to her in 1927.[96] In anthropology, Ruth Benedict and Margaret Mead added their fruitful contributions to their field.

Perhaps the area where women teachers met the most searing disappointment was in their relationship to the public. The negative stereotype of the professor—a seedy, absent-minded, weak individual living in an unrealistic world—was exceeded only by those of women professors. "We seldom pick up a magazine today that we do not find ourselves discussed—practically always with derogatory epithets," bemoaned Marjorie Nicholson, Assistant Professor of English at Goucher College.[97] The brunt of the negative comment fell on the female teachers of women's colleges. Often they were pictured as embittered spinsters who had turned to teaching because they failed in life or love. An article in *Harper's Magazine* commented:

> I do not suggest, of course, that even a majority of the instructors in women's colleges have a forbidding personality; but it is probable that, taken as a whole, they are distinctly lacking in physical attractiveness, charm of manner, and social agreeableness. . . .Perhaps these personal disadvantages are inseparable from the teaching profession—or rather the women's half of the teaching profession.[98]

Eugenicists and others blamed women for the low rate of marriage and motherhood among the graduates of women's colleges, those believed most capable of maintaining the American race because of their superior intellect, culture, and social background. Academic women were accused of pushing their students, whose undivided attention they controlled, towards careers at a time when the girls should have been falling in love.[99]   While it was true that only 11 percent of all women college teachers were married, it was questionable that they influenced the marriage or birth rate of their students.[100]

In a society that valued education as a preparation for an individual's life-work rather than as a search for knowledge, women teachers, many of whom belonged to a generation of pioneers in education, did not fit.[101] Although they advanced within their disciplines and in the teaching profession as a whole, they knew deep disappointment in failing to reach their students, the blase youth of the twenties.

In each of the three professions, special conditions affected women's opportunities for advancement. Medicine was moving in the direction of greater specialization and the reliance on hospitals and diagnostic equipment. Women physicians had difficulty obtaining advanced training necessary for specialization and hospital affiliation. They were consequently forced into certain peripheral practices and careers. Because women lawyers were so new to the profession, they found they had little to offer prospective employers. More so than women doctors, female attorneys had to fight a negative stereotype and convince the profession and the public that women could be competent lawyers. Of the three groups, academic women fared the best. Besides being blessed with an expanding educational market and a traditional place in the profession, female teachers had fine women's colleges where they found ample opportunity to manifest their abilities without threatening and competing with men.

In all of the professions, women ran into common problems. They found that competence was not enough: women had to be far better than men to advance within their fields. Men dominated each profession and determined, to some extent, who would reach the top. Except in a minority of cases, men tended to belittle or ignore the contributions that women did make. In one of her speeches to the National Association of Women Lawyers, President Emilie M. Bullowa summarized the conditions for women in the legal profession in a way that applied to medicine and higher education as well:

> The gates barred against us because of prejudice against the new order of things have, indeed, been unlocked, but the hinges, by long disuse, have become rusted, and they do not yet swing fully open. We get through with but great effort.[102]

NOTES

[1]The only source to tabulate graduates of law schools by sex was the "Biennial Survey of Education" of the Bureau of Education. The figures for non-reporting years were arrived at by interpolation. See Tables 2, 4, and 6 in the Appendix for a summary of graduation staistics.

[2]Bertha Van Hoosen, "Opportunities for Medical Women Interns," *MWJ* 33 (March, 1926), 65.

[3]Quoted in Bertha Van Hoosen, "Opportunities for Medical Women Interns," *MWJ* 33 (April, 1926), 103.

[4]Idem, "Opportunities for Medical Women Interns," *MWJ* 33 (May, 1926), 126-128.

[5]Quoted in "Ambulance Rider," *Woman's Journal* 13 (January, 1928), 19.

[6]The male physicians and administrators did not present any statistics to support their assumptions. Bertha Van Hoosen, "Quo Vadis?" *MWJ* 36 (January, 1929), 2.

[7]There was a higher percentage of married women among women physicians than either among women professionals as a group or among all working women. *1920 Census*, 4:697-698; *1930 Census*, 4:69, 73.

[8]Martha Tracy, "Women Graduates in Medicine," *AAMC Bulletin* 2 (January, 1927), 23.

[9]Florence DeL. Lowther and Helen R. Downes, "Women in Medicine," *JAMA* 129 (October 13, 1945), 512-514.

[10]Ibid., Van Hoosen, "Quo Vadis?" 2.

[11]Dr. Tracy found that 90 percent of her sample had taken internships. Tracy, 23. By the end of the decade, the AMA estimated that 95 percent of all medical graduates took a year of internship. "Medical Education in the U.S.: Editorial," *JAMA* 93 (August 17, 1929), 547-548.

[12]*1920 Census*, 4:56-127; *1930 Census*, 4:112-1788.

[13]Martha Tracy, "Women in Medicine," *AAMC Bulletin* 3 (October, 1928), 327.

[14]H. G. Weiskotten, "A Study of Present Tendencies in Medical Practice," *AAMC Bulletin* 3 (April, 1928), 135.

[15]Weiskotten, 135.

[16]Tracy, "Women in Medicine," 328. By the 1940's, the top preferences for women had changed to pediatrics, psychiatry, obstetrics and gynecology, and internal medicine. Lowther and Downes, 513.

[17]"Women in Medicine," *Saturday Evening Post* 200 (January 21, 1928), 22; Inez C. Philbrick, "Women, Let Us Be Loyal to Women," *WMJ* 36 (February, 1929), 41.

[18]Sara Josephine Baker, *Fighting for Life* (New York: Macmillan Company, 1939), 52.

[19]Dr. Anna E. Rude, Director of the Division of Hygiene, U. S. Children's Bureau, estimated that, in 1920, only 13.6 percent of all births in the United States occurred in hospitals. Anna E. Rude, "The Sheppard-Towner Bill in Relation to Public Health," *JAMA* 79 (September 16, 1922), 962.

[20]Bertha Van Hoosen, "Opportunities for Medical Women Interns," *MWJ* 33 (December, 1926), 342-343.

[21]There were 5,272 male and female doctors in Manhattan in 1920 and 5,217 males and 409 females in 1930. *1920 Census*, 4:1173; *1930 Census*, 4:1142-1143.

[22]"Gotham Hospital," *MWJ* 36 (April, 1929), 89.

[23]Ibid., *MWJ* 33 (April, 1926), 111.

[24]Bertha Van Hoosen, "Opportunities for Women to Do Research in Medicine," *MWJ* 37 (June, 1930), 162.

[25]"United We Stand," *MWJ* 28 (April, 1921), 100.

[26]Bertha Van Hoosen, "Do Women Doctors Need their Own Medical Journal?" *MWJ* 36 (January, 1929), 16.

[27]Bertha Van Hoosen, "Medical Opportunities for Women," *MWJ* 34 (June, 1927), 173.

[28]Alice Hamilton, *Exploring the Dangerous Trades* (Boston: Little Brown, 1943), 252.

[29]Baker, 189-191.

[30]Hamilton.

[31]Bertha Van Hoosen, *Petticoat Surgeon* (Chicago: Pelligini and Cudahy, 1947), 198-199.

[32]Elinor Bluemel, *Florence Sabin: Colorado Woman of the Century* (Bolder: University of Colorado Press, 1959), 87.

[33]Bertha Van Hoosen, "Report of the Committee on Medical Opportunities for Women," *MWJ* 35 (July, 1928), 198.

[34]Baker, 201; Ethel M. Watters, "Child Hygiene and the Sheppard-Towner Fund," *Southern Medical Journal* 17 (March, 1924), 189-190.

[35]Adams, *Women Professional Workers*, 69.

[36]Harold Florian Clark, *Life Earnings in Selected Occupations in the United States* (New York: Harper and Brothers, 1937), 70.

[37]Margaret Elliott and Grace E. Manson, *Earnings of Women in Business and the Professions* (Ann Arbor: University of Michigan School of Business, Bureau of Business Research, 1930), 56-57.

[38]Harry H. Moore, "Health and Medical Practice," in *Recent Social Trends in the United States*, 1104-1105; Tracy, "Women Graduates in Medicine," 27.

[39]Bertha Van Hoosen, "Opportunities for Medical Women Interns," *MWJ* 33 (December, 1926), 342.

[40]"Shall Medical Women Hold Official Positions in the AMA?" *MWJ* 34 (October, 1927), 288; "The Boston Meeting," *MWJ* 28 (June, 1921), 147; "Report of the Tenth Medical Women's National Association Convention," *MWJ* 31 (July, 1924), 197.

[41]"The Boston Meeting," 147; "Report of the Tenth Medical Women's National Association Convention," 197.

[42]Bertha Van Hoosen, "Report of the Committee on Medical Opportunities for Women," *MWJ* 35 (July, 1928), 198-199.

[43]Idem, "Women Doctors as Members of Medical Societies," *MWJ* 36 (October, 1929), 276; "Would it Were True," *MWJ* 35 (August, 1928), 232.

[44]Ibid.; "Sex Prejudice Among the Doctors," *WC* 6 (July 2, 1921), 15.

[45]Carleton B. Chapman, "*The Flexner Report* by Abraham Flexner," *Daedalus* 103 (Winter, 1974), 105-117.

[46]The *MWJ* carried regular reports on the activities of American Women's Hospitals, particularly in the early years of the decade. *Index Medicus*, the *Reader's Guide* of medical literature, had no citations for this organization during the twenties. See also Martha Welpton, "Women Physicians," *Journal of the Michigan Medical Society* 50 (May, 1931), 341-342.

[47]At the end of the 1920's, articles on women medical missionaries in China and India appeared regularly in the *MWJ*. The only other medical journal to carry much information on the subject was the *Journal of Chinese Medicine*, which was published by medical missionaries. Hamilton, 311.

[48]Morris Fishbein, *A History of the American Medical Association*, 1847-1947 (Philadelphia: W.B. Saunders Company, 1947), 330-331.

[49]The Medical Women's National Association passed a resolution favoring the Sheppard-Towner Bill in June, 1921. *MWJ* 28 (June, 1921), 150. When the AMA passed a resolution against it the following June, an article in the *MWJ* commented: "We regret the action of the House of Delegates upon the Sheppard-Towner Act, and

we fail to understand the position of the medical Profession at large upon the subject of prohibition, if the House of Delegates represents it correctly." "The AMA Meeting in St. Louis," *MWJ* 29 (June, 1922), 120.

[50]Quoted in C. W. Lillie, "What Shall We Do To Be Saved—Professionally?" *Illinois Medical Journal* 42 (July, 1922), 30.

[51]The author found no negative statements on the Sheppard-Towner Bill by women physicians. Of the medical journals, *MWJ* provided the most information on the bill and the subsequent activities arising from its implementation.

[52]The number of male graduates was approximately 63,479 and the number of male lawyers rose by 36,439. *1930 Census,* 5:47.

[53]*1920 Census,* 4:56-127.

[54]*Women Lawyers' Journal* 12 (August, 1923), 30 (hereafter cited as *WLJ*).

[55]Interview with Margaret J. Carns, February 3, 1920, BVI Papers, Box 10, Law Interviews with Women Lawyers.

[56]Interview with Sophonisba Breckinridge, February 21, 1920, BVI Papers, Box 10, Law: Interviews with Women Lawyers.

[57]Questionnaire No. 229, March 15, 1920, BVI Papers, Box 10, Law: Questionnaires from Women Lawyers.

[58]Henrietta Dunlop Stonestreet, "The Women Lawyers in Maryland," *WLJ* 15 (July, 1927), 8.

[59]Jean H. Norris, "Women in the Law," in Doris E. Fleischman, ed., *An Outline of Careers for Women: A Practical Guide to Achievement* (Garden City, N.Y.: Doubleday, Doran and Company, 1928), 272.

[60]*WLJ* 12 (August, 1923), 30.

[61]Hatcher, *Occupations for Women,* 339.

[62]Questionnaire No. 227, n.d., BVI Papers, Box 10, Law: Questionnaires for Women Lawyers in Business.

[63]Ellen Spencer Mussey, "Women Attorneys," *ABAJ* 9 (January, 1923), 63.

[64]Alice Boarman Baldridge, "Are Women Free?" *WC* 7 (February 24, 1923), 24.

[65]Norris, 280.

[66]Lawyer Rosalie F. Janoer summed up the situation for women in the profession: "We might as well be fair with ourselves, and that, regardless of what might be said,

the fact remains that the woman lawyer represents no big business." Rosalie F. Janoer, "The Practicing Woman Lawyer's Needs," *WLJ* 9 (February, 1920), 12.

[67] H. S. Richards to Emma P. Hirth, November 20, 1919, BVI Papers, Box 11, Law: Letters from Law Schools.

[68] Hatcher, 340-342.

[69] Harold Florian Clark, 62.

[70] Doerschuck, *Women in the Law*, 57.

[71] Elliott and Manson, 56.

[72] Grace Irene Rohleder, "Some Reasons Why Women Should Study Law and Practice the Profession," *WLJ* 13 (April, 1924), 15.

[73] "Women Members of the American Bar Association," *WLJ* 15 (January, 1927), 3-4; *WLJ* 15 (October, 1927), 11-12.

[74] "Women Members of the American Bar Association," 3; The *Index to Legal Periodicals* showed few articles by women lawyers.

[75] In 1927, six women were appointed to local councils of the ABA. *WLJ* 15 (October, 1927), 12; Julia M. Alexander was elected vice-president of the North Carolina State Bar Association in 1924. *WLJ* 13 (June, 1924), 2; "Address of Emilie M. Bullowa," *WLJ* 13 (October, 1924), 5.

[76] *WLJ* 10 (April, 1921), 21.

[77] "Judge Mary O'Toole," *WC* 6 (August 13, 1921), 20; Mildred Adams, "First on the Federal Bench: Katherine Sellers, Judge of the Juvenile Court of Washington, D.C.," *WC* 9 (April 4, 1925), 12, 24-25; Mussey, 62-63; *WLJ* 13 (January, 1924), 11.

[78] "The Blanket Equality Bill," *WLJ* 12 (December, 1922-January, 1923), 12-13; Reba Talbot Swain, "Our Attitude on Legislation," *WLJ* 12 (October-November, 1922), 5; Emilie M. Bullowa, "Address," *WLJ* 13 (January, 1924), 10; Rose Falls Bres, "Shall There Be Special Restrictive Laws for Women?" *WLJ* 15 (July, 1927), 4.

[79] Preliminary Report of Committee W on the Status of Women in College and University Faculties," *AAUP Bulletin* 7 (October, 1921), 21, 24.

[80] "Preliminary Report of Committee W on the Status of Women in College and University Faculties," *AAUP Bulletin* 7 (October, 1921), 21, 23.

[81] The best way to find out the subjects that women frequently taught is to examine old college catalogues that listed faculty members. Another excellent source is the *AAUP Bulletin* which listed prospective members, their institutions, and their departments. "Preliminary Report of Committee W," 23.

[82]Trevor Arnett, *Teachers' Salaries in Certain Endowed and State Supported Colleges and Universities in the United States with Special Reference to Colleges of Arts, Literature, and Science, 1926-1927*, Publication of the General Education Board, *Occasional Papers*, No. 8 (1928), 11.

[83]"Preliminary Report of Committee W," 26-27.

[84]Ibid., 27.

[85]Marcus W. Jernegan, "Productivity of Doctors of Philosophy in History," *American Historical Review* 33 (October, 1927), 1-22; "The Question of Women's Colleges," *Atlantic Monthly* 140 (November, 1927), 577-584.

[86]"Second Report of Committee W on the Status of Women in College and University Faculties," *AAUP Bulletin* 10 (November, 1924), 65-72; Ella Lonn, "Academic Status of Women on University Faculties," *AAUW Journal* 17 (January-March, 1924), 5-19.

[87]Lonn, 5-19. The AAUP Study showed that a considerable number of female students also preferred men teachers because the girls could fool them more easily than they could women teachers. "Second Report of Committee W," 69.

[88]Lonn, 10.

[89]"Second Report of Committee W," 66-72.

[90]Lonn, 6.

[91]Lonn, 7.

[92]It should be remembered that in surveys made by mailing out questionnaires, usually those who have been successful are more likely to respond than those who have not succeeded. Emilie J. Hutchinson, "Women and the Ph.D.," *AAUW Journal* 22 (October, 1928), 21.

[93]Ibid., 21.

[94]On the Council were: Lucy M. Salmon, Vassar (1920); Ellen C. Hinsdale, Mt. Holyoke (1920); Marian P. Whitney, Vassar (1921-1922, 1926); Mary W. Calkins, Wellsley (1925); Eunice M. Schenk, Bryn Mawr (1926-1929); Katherine Gallagher, Goucher (1927-1929); Elizabeth R. Laird, Mt. Holyoke (1928-1930). Heads of Committees included: Florence Bascomb, Bryn Mawr (1921-1925); Lucile Eaves, Simmons (1922-1930); Marian P. Whitney (1929-1930). The vice-presidents were Marian P. Whitney and Mary W. Calkins.

[95]Tables of contents in each journal supplied the information. The percentages are approximations since some of the names do not reveal the sex of their owners and many authors gave first initials only.

[96]Washburn Commemorative Volume of the *Amercan Journal of Psychology* 39 (December, 1927).

[97]Marjorie Nicolson, "Scholars and Ladies," *Yale Review* n.s. 19 (June, 1930), 776.

[98]R. LeClerc Phillips, "The Problem of the Education Woman," *Harper's Magazine* 154 (December, 1926), 58-59.

[99]Ibid.; Summary of a speech by Louis I. Dublin entitled "The Higher Education of Women and Race Betterment," made at the National Eugenics Conference, September 26, 1921, BVI Papers, Box 21, Scientific Work: Biology and Botany; Meyrick Booth, *Woman and Society* (New York: Longmans, Green and Company, 1929), 11-12.

[100]*1920 Census*, 4:697-698; *1930 Census*, 4:59, 73.

[101]Bessie Bunzel, "Woman Goes to College," *Century Magazine* 117 (November, 1928), 30-32; Louis I. Dublin, *Health and Wealth* (New York: Harper and Brothers, 1928), 238, 243; James M. Wood, "The Challenge of the Twentieth Century," *WC* 8 (February 23, 1924), 10.

[102]"Address of Emilie M. Bullowa," 5.

CHAPTER V

THE DILEMMA OF THE PROFESSIONAL WOMAN

Despite the removal of many barriers in the twenties, few professional women would have claimed that they stood on an equal footing with their male colleagues. Only females of extraordinary abilities received much recognition, and most of that resulted from their position as women of achievement in a masculine environment. The majority of professional women concentrated in subordinate positions with low pay and few opportunities for advancement. While many women wanted to improve their status in these occupations, disagreement over how to achieve equality split the feminine ranks. The controversy focused on whether or not women should exploit their minority status; should women, in the feminist tradition, band together and demand better conditions for themselves, or should they quietly accept the recent advances and try to blend in with the men? The polarization appeared most clearly in the activities of and reactions to the women's professional organizations.

While it was true that women in all three professions experienced similar problems, those in higher education appeared to have had a more firmly established position than their sisters in medicine or law. Perhaps because they had a traditional place in the profession and had participated in the AAUP from its birth, women teachers did not feel a need for their own organization or their own professional journal. The associations they did form were usually based on individual disciplines, rather than teaching, and were of limited scope in terms of goals and activities.[1] In medicine and law, however, female practitioners were fully aware of their subordinate status, and they used their organizations to improve it.

Both women lawyers and women doctors had to answer some difficult questions. In the first place, regardless of their motivation for doing so, these women had chosen high-level occupations which derived at least part of their prestige from their masculine character. Some women apparently thought that a large increase in the number of female practitioners would diminish the prestige of the profession and, consequently, their own.[2] Furthermore, the act of selecting medicine or law, particularly in view of the long training period and personal sacrifices involved signified the willingness of women to accept the conditions and mores of the professions. At the same time, women could not shake off their sex, their visible mark as a minority group in the professions. No matter how many speeches they made, professional women realized that the men in their fields continued to see them as females first and doctors or lawyers second. Should women protest this situation or ignore it? Did male and female practitioners differ in their abilities and interests? Did women have an obligation to their sex as well as to their profession? Some women turned to their own professional organizations for answers.

Women usually formed their own occupational societies because the regular associations, dominated by men, either flatly denied them membership or effectively excluded them from the power structure.[3] As a minority group, professional women needed the support and encouragement a group of likeminded individuals could give. Through their journals and newsletters, they kept in touch with each other, voiced opinions on a variety of topics, and published technical articles which other professional journals were reluctant to accept. Societies gave women a sense of identity as well as an instrument for carrying out their own programs.[4]

Medical women followed the common pattern when they established the American Medical Women's Association. Female doctors attended and attempted to participate in the annual meetings of the AMA for years before they finally won official membership in 1915. Their early experiences were filled with frustration. In 1909, Dr. Rosalie Slaughter Morton, a prominent New York surgeon, suggested that the impromptu talks on health and hygiene that female doctors gave to women's clubs be formalized into a lecture bureau sponsored by the AMA and run by women. The idea met with ridicule and attempts to block it, but the Public Health and Education Committee went into action anyhow. Although the official history of the AMA subsequently claimed that the committee had no right to exist, it was so successful that its activities were eventually absorbed by the powerful Council on Health and Public Education, the public relations branch of the AMA.[5] At the same time, Dr. Bertha Van Hoosen began organizing banquets for women doctors at the AMA conventions because they were often excluded from the dinners of the various Sections. In 1915, Dr. Van Hoosen and some Chicago colleagues decided to form a national women's medical society which emerged the next year as the American Medical Women's Association with Dr. Van Hoosen as its first president. The organization changed its name to the Medical Women's National Association (MWNA) in 1919.

The time was hardly auspicious for the formation of a women's medical society. Despite riding the wave of general feminist activity, the birth of the MWNA coincided with formal recognition of women as members of the AMA. Many female doctors objected to an attempt to continue segregation at a time when better conditions seemed just over the horizon.[6] Had it not been for America's involvement in World War I and the Surgeon General's refusal of the volunteer services of five thousand women doctors, the organization would probably have died.[7] The Surgeon's actions, interpreted as an insult to women physicians, acted as a catalyst. Women doctors of the West coast, among the strongest opponents of the MWNA, began a petition protesting this discrimination, and they asked the Association to present it to the Surgeon General. Stung into action, women physicians launched the American Women's Hospitals (AWH) in war-torn areas throughout Europe under the auspices of the MWNA and ably directed by Drs. Morton and Van Hoosen. The AWH first established hospitals during the war and then later continued relief work in distressed areas during the twenties.[8] The organization maintained a volunteer list of more than a thousand women doctors, many of whom provided their skills without pay.

While no one doubted the importance of the humanitarian enterprise, the AWH proved an insufficient reason for maintaining a separate professional organization for women following the Armistice. With the battle for suffrage won, women composing ever larger proportions of medical classes, and many earlier restrictions disintegrating in the early twenties, some female doctors renewed their objections to the MWNA. Since it maintained the same standards for admission as the AMA, membership in the women's organization conferred no special distinction, only extra dues.[9] The main argument against the association was that it served no function and only increased the segregation of the sexes within the profession. To many women physicians, the gains of the preceding years were satisfactory, and they resented activities that might neutralize their benefits. Apparently, the opponents of the Association won converts because the number of dues-paying members dropped from six hundred in 1921 to 350 in 1926.[10]

Despite a membership, real or nominal, of under a thousand during the decade, some of the most active, outstanding, and vocal women in the profession belonged to the MWNA. Drs. Bertha Van Hoosen, Florence Sabin, Josephine Baker, and Eliza M. Mosher were only a few of the stellar members who participated in the organization. Since many of the leading members of the society were veterans of the suffrage and other campaigns who understood the value of concerted effort, they tried ceaselessly to lure recalcitrant women into the fold. In her presidential address in 1920, Dr. Martha Tracy tried to assuage the doubts of non-members;

> We exist, not for segregation from medical men in scientific work, but as machinery to accomplish certain things in the interest of women to which men have given scant attention, and must be done by women, if done at all.[11]

Not only did Dr.Tracy want to promote opportunities for women in the professions, but also she advocated the development of more distinctive projects similar to the American Women's Hospitals. She contended that, individually and in cooperation with other women's groups, female doctors should work for legislation safeguarding the health of their sex and of children.[12]   Dr. Tracy's speech highlighted the two dominant themes for the MWNA program during the 1920's: improved conditions for women in medicine and involvement in issues of interest to their sex.

While opportunities for women physicians apparently continued to expand in the early twenties, the exhortations of the *MWJ*, the mouthpiece for the MWNA, retained a special quality. Editorials and articles recognized the existence of sexual prejudice and its effects in the world of medicine but did not dwell on them. Instead, writers blamed women for not capitalizing on their ever growing opportunities. When no women appeared as members of the AMA House of Delegates in 1921, an article asked,

> Was that our fault as medical women or was it the fault of some one else? At all events, the fault . . . lies "back home," and not in the House of Delegates. If we fail to make our judgment, personality and scientific ability felt in our state society, there is no reason for accrediting us to the National body.[13]

As to the small number of females presenting papers at the convention, the author commented; "Are we so meagerly represented because we have nothing to say, or because we don't know how to say it, or because we do not seek the opportunity?"[14]   The leaders of the MWNA suggested that women's lack of initiative and complacency might be part of the problem. Warning their sisters against being lulled into a false sense of security, the leaders urged them to keep alive the pioneer spirit. But other than general remonstrations, the MWNA had no concrete program for removing women from their subordinate status in the medical profession.

With only a vague idea of what kind of problems faced them, medical women were handicapped when they tried to develop a plan of action. Knowledge of the existence of discrimination in education and practice was insufficient; the women needed to back up their statements with concrete statistics and conceptions of how the mechanism of discrimination worked. Rare, indeed, were the articles such as the one describing how sexual discrimination was built into the laws governing civil service appointments. The author ended with the following plea: "It is high time women physicians as a class recognized this situation, and worked for legislation to remove the discriminations which restrict their activities in the field of medicine."[15] Other writers, however, did not amplify this theme. As long as women doctors continued to think that conditions were improving for them in the field, there was little incentive for them to discover the extent of sexual discrimination or ways to eliminate it.

By mid-decade, a growing number of medical women realized that the outlook for their sex in the profession was not as rosy as they had once supposed. Both the proportion and the number of female medical students declined after 1922 and 1923.[16] Recurrent complaints about the difficulty women physicians faced in securing internships, residencies, or hospital appointments could not be ignored. Despite the growing popularity of medicine as a career among young men, interest among young women appeared to be waning. At a vocational conference for college women, Dr. Florence Brown Sherbon, President of the Kansas Medical Women's Association, learned that girls shied away from medical careers because of the expense, the incompatibility of marriage and career, and the continued sexual prejudice in the field.[17] The situation called for some kind of action, and the MWNA even had an instrument, largely inactive, in the Committee on Opportunities for Women in Medicine. When Bertha Van Hoosen assumed control of the committee in 1925, however, it started a whirlwind of activity.

Dr. Van Hoosen, an energetic and peppery woman who was a born fighter, directed the numerous, enlightening surveys on all aspects of women in the medical profession that appeared in the *MWJ* during the twenties. Since a key obstacle was the lack of internships for women, Dr. Van Hoosen spent a year finding which hospitals accepted women and why others did not. She evaluated the advantages and disadvantages of women's, Catholic, and Jewish hospitals and discussed the special problems that black women doctors would encounter. Dr. Van Hoosen gave young women sound advice on how to distinguish between good and bad programs and how to apply for them. One of the most important features of the series was the list of hospitals willing to accept female interns if only they would apply.[18] The series undoubtedly helped young women find internships by providing them with the guidance that many coeducational schools did not. In like manner, the Committee on Opportunities discovered how women fared in the fields of research, teaching, and institutional work.[19] The whole process of selection of medical students came under scrutiny, and the Committee kept track of women's participation in medical societies.[20] By the end of the decade, hardly an aspect of the problems facing women in medicine had not been examined by Van Hoosen and company.

In conjunction with the fact-finding of the Committee on Opportunities, the MWNA began taking a more positive and aggressive stance. The programs and resolutions approved at the annual meetings pinpointed trouble spots. In the area of education, for example, the MWNA established a loan fund for deserving students and advocated the use of national entrance exams that would not discriminate against female applicants. Since only the Women's Medical College had women representatives on its admissions committee, the Association recommended that all coeducational institutions do likewise. The leaders denounced the trend developing in many schools at the end off the decade of intimidating female students by admitting only one per class.[21] With the same kind of thoroughness, the MWNA protested against sexual discrimination in hospitals, training programs, and medical societies. The members advocated the use of civil service examinations for appointments in all publicly supported hospitals, and they lobbied Congress to change existing laws that barred women doctors from the military and higher ranks of government service.[22] By the end of the twenties, the Association had identified a number of key areas to attack.

Because women composed an uninfluential minority group within the medical profession, their protests had small impact on the institution other than publicizing existing injustices. Dr. Inez C. Philbrick explained summarily that "Men do not want women in their institutions and organizations except as subordinates and auxiliaries."[23] In the past, women had found full opportunities only in their own schools and hospitals, and female physicians called for renewed support of such facilities in the twenties. When financial strain nearly caused the Women's Medical College to close in the early twenties, alumnae and non-medical women raised enough money to keep the school open and even build a new home for it.[24] Similarly, a proposal to merge the only women's hospital in New York City with the Columbia University Hospital, which would decrease staff positions for female doctors, aroused angry protests from the medical sisterhood of the city. To fill the predicted hole left by the expected merger, female physicians developed a blueprint for a new women's hospital that would run on a non-profit basis.[25] In Chicago and Detroit as well, women doctors enlarged or improved their own hospitals.[26] Female doctors were urged to rely on their professional sisters for referrals and consultations, and to make this suggestion feasible, the MWNA published its first directory of women doctors in 1928.[27] Since women often found medical journals reluctant to accept their technical articles, the MWJ stepped into the breech and provided them with opportunities to publish. By creating their own opportunities and solutions, women doctors managed to circumvent some of the existing inequities.

Not content with trying to widen opportunities for medical women, the members of the MWNA also wanted to put their indelible imprint on the profession by making contributions as women. Dr. Florence Sherbon told female medical students that women no longer had to prove that they could do anything men could do; the time had come for them to contribute something to the medical field as women.[28] Emphasizing the difference in interests between the sexes and the many areas within medicine needing improvement, Dr. Kate Campbell Mead pointed out that

> Men take up these reforms in one way and women in another. Neither is perhaps wholly capable of completing the business alone; and therefore what is offered by medical women in large and competent groups will be accepted, although perhaps with as much surprise as was shown when medical women opened hospitals and did hard work during the war.29

Considering the existing conditions in the medical profession and the fact that several of the leaders of the MWNA had participated in the suffrage movement, it was not unusual that medical women chose to make their contribution in the fields of health care for women and children. More than a few thought that these areas "belonged" to women physicians and that they should therefore become the "guardians of the race."[30]

The desire to help their sex and children involved the members of the Association in some controversial issues and programs. The AMA condemned the Sheppard-Towner Act as creeping socialism, but the MWNA supported it whole-heartedly throughout the twenties. Nor was it out of character for the organization to pass resolutions supporting the Child Labor Amendment.[31] In order to protect future generations and women from the ravages of venereal disease, women doctors launched an educational campaign on social hygiene. Their most daring activity, however, was their involvement in the birth control movement. In the first half of the decade, the pages of *MWJ* carried ringing articles on both sides of the question, partly because Eliza M. Mosher, senior editor, was unalterably opposed to any form of birth control. After 1925, when Dr. Mosher died, the articles shifted in favor of contraception under doctors' supervision. The women argued that birth control would help preserve the American race, a reason acceptable to many people who believed in eugenics.[32] Since birth control was illegal for most of the decade in the United States, women doctors found that, no matter how they approached the topic, they were likely to be in the center of a heated debate.

The issues the women chose to support were calculated to alienate much of the profession and the laity as well. No matter how forward-looking the organization appeared with hind-sight, the MWNA earned a reputation of radicalism in the 1920's. The AMA and MWNA were on opposite sides concerning the Sheppard-Towner Act, and although many men agreed with their sisters on the subject of contraception, they were sometimes reluctant to say so.[33] Some of the women espoused radical ideas. Both Inez C. Philbrick and Josephine Baker upheld the idea of socialized medicine, but for different reasons. Dr. Philbrick believed women doctors would be unable to compete with men as long as the profession remained on a competitive commercial basis, while Dr. Baker thought that only under state medicine would the masses receive adequate health care.[34] Naturally, such opinions struck fear into the hearts of conservative physicians.

Because of the radical mien of the MWNA, it is not surprising that the majority of women doctors avoided association with it. They were unwilling to jeopardize the visible, if limited, gains women had made in medicine in the early twenties by making more demands. The resulting small size of the society limited its effectiveness in winning improvements for women doctors. Nor could the organization compete with regular societies in terms of intellectual stimulation or prestige. To many women physicians, female solidarity meant female isolation, something they had been trying to overcome for years. The MWNA was more successful in launching programs and winning support for issues such as the Sheppard-Towner Bill and birth control than it was in improving the status of women in the medical profession. Without the support of all women doctors, the Association could not fight the power structure of the profession in the twenties.

Women lawyers formed their own professional organization because local and national bar associations had excluded them. More than its medical counterpart, however, the National Association of Women Lawyers (NAWL) was plagued by small size and a late start. Founded originally as a local organization in 1899, the Women Lawyers Association of New York City grew slowly as it gradually extended membership to women attorneys in other states. By the twenties, other states with large metropolitan areas and many women lawyers had formed similar societies. In 1923, the New York Association decided to become officially a national group: with over 2,500 women in the profession, it finally seemed as if there were enough prospective members to make such an organization feasible.[35]

The leaders of the NAWL, aware of the shakiness of their organization, tried continually to enlist new members. Unlike the AMA and MWNA, which had identical standards for admission, the NAWL had fewer requirements for membership than the state or national bar associations. To belong to the ABA, a lawyer had to be a member in good standing of her local bar for three years prior to her application. In contrast, the NAWL accepted women as soon as they passed their bar exams.[36] The women's organization recruited young attorneys when they were most enthusiastic and when they were most likely to need fellowship and encouragement. On the other hand, the NAWL was not constructed along federal lines: membership in a state women lawyers' society did not automatically confer membership in the national body. Because most women lawyers wanted to join their local bar societies and the ABA and because a local women's society, rather than a distant national organization, often met the special needs of women attorneys, the NAWL had to compete with other organizations for members. At no time during the twenties did its membership reach five hundred.[37] When officials raised the annual dues from three to five dollars in 1927, membership dropped precipitously and the organization ceased publication of its magazine, the *Women Lawyers' Journal (WLJ)* between July, 1928 and January, 1930.[38]

The women lawyers' organization had a difficult time justifying its existence, which partially accounted for its small membership. One female attorney observed that opponents were divided into two groups: those who saw no reason whatsoever for the NAWL and those who saw no vital need for it but would belong as long as it existed.[39] The adversaries reasoned that, because women had been members of the ABA since 1918 and local bar associations were opening their doors as well, a separate organization for women was anachronistic. The NAWL merely emphasized women's isolation from the profession and tended to perpetuate the term "women lawyers."[40] Luke-warm members agreed but pointed out the positive value of fellowship. In a speech to the male-dominated Michigan Bar Association, Theresa Doland, member of the Michigan Women Lawyers' Association, tried to explain the function of her organization:

> I want to say right here the spirit of the age among progressive women is to get away from women's associations simply because of their being women's associations. They are living in an age when that is no longer necessary except for social purposes.[41]

Many women lawyers thought that ideally the NAWL would gradually fade away as the regular associations accepted women as fully equal members.[42]

The women who gave their whole-hearted support to the Association were not optimistic about the future of their sex in local and national bar societies. As a visible minority group, they realized that they would be called "women lawyers" willy nilly. "It is doubtful if we shall be called otherwise for many years. We should be happy that we are not always dubbed 'lady lawyers' or 'modern Portias,'" commented one article in the WLJ.[43] Women's acceptance in regular societies, albeit courteous, was merely token: only a few women held minor or honorary offices.[44] While it was important to belong to the ABA, it was also quite clear that women would have little say in its policies. An editorial in the WLJ pointed out that "It is well to join men's law associations as a side issue, but the progressive work for women lawyers must be done by women's organizations."[45] The leaders of the NAWL envisioned an active association that would improve the status of women in the legal profession.

Several obstacles prevented women from achieving their goal, however. The luke-warm members who valued the organization for its social purposes were so much dead weight when it came to formulating programs. The small size and lack of money made even limited surveys, similar to those of the MWNA, unfeasible.[46] Consequently, female attorneys remained ignorant of how many women practiced law in the United States, which positions were open to women, and how to secure them. The NAWL periodically made suggestions such as increasing the number of women on the bench, opening more approved schools to coeducation, or endowing special chairs to be filled by women teachers.[47] On the other hand, the Association had no scholarship or loan fund of its own during the twenties.[48] Although the WLJ carried news items about women in the profession and served as a forum for debate on issues of interest to the members, it contained little else. Reprinted speeches from various meetings vied for space with a few technical articles, some of which had male authors.[49] The membership included some of the most prominent women lawyers and judges, but the Association lacked dynamic leadership.

The irresolution that characterized the NAWL inhibited the organization from developing clear-cut policies on a variety of issues. As was true of their medical sisters, many women attorneys felt obligated to continue the work of the woman's movement. Certainly existing laws on marriage and divorce, equal pay, citizenship, jury duty, and child labor were enough to keep them busy.[50] Such plans, however, met with strong opposition. Emilie M. Bullowa, President of the Association from 1921 to 1924, warned, "We do not want to exhaust our energy on women's or even children's legislation."[51] She counselled members to broaden their interests, reminding them that all laws made by men affected women. From a different and purely legal perspective, some of the women attorneys objected to the form that the proposed reforms often took—Constitutional Amendments. Attempts to win support for the Child Labor Amendment aroused a barrage of negative comments and, in the end, the NAWL took no action on the subject.[52]

Hampered by vacillation and disunity, the Association was slow to develop a sense of purpose. The issue that crystalized the goals of the organization was the Equal Rights Amendment, also known as the Blanket Equality Bill. When the idea first appeared in 1922, the members of the Women Lawyers' Association debated its pros and cons.[53] The major speaker against the bill said that a federal law was unnecessary for a problem which she thought was limited primarily to the South. Her remarks were seconded by Helen McCormick, Assistant District Attorney for Kings County, New York:

> American women have the right to express their convictions in their vote, and if they are unable to bring about any reforms necessary in the laws then there is something wrong with American women.[54]

Paula Ladey had obtained her information on the Blanket Equality Bill from the National Women's Party, sponsor of the bill, and she was an enthusiastic convert. The bill, she noted, would help women in general but, for women in the law, it would mean an end of discrimination in publicly supported law schools and government positions. Reba Talbot Swain, head of the legislative committee of the Association, identified the trouble spot. If the Blanket Equality Bill became law, protective legislation for women would be invalidated.[55] Were women lawyers willing to improve their own status at the expense of other groups of women?

Throughout the rest of the decade, the question of protective legislation versus equal rights worried the NAWL. A subtle shift in favor of equal rights gradually became noticeable, however. In 1925, the adverse reaction to the Child Labor Amendment in the *WLJ* heralded the change. Articles on the legal status of women concentrated on removing inequities rather than on the need for laws shortening the work day. But as long as protective legislation did not affect women lawyers themselves, they did not develop a strategy against it.[56] In 1927, however, the California legislature tried to enact an eight-hour day for all working women, including those in the professions. Interpreting this proposal as a threat to their ability to compete with men, female attorneys joined with other women's organizations to defeat the bill.[57] In the aftermath of the California campaign, the NAWL passed a resolution condemning all protective laws that did not apply equally to both sexes and enjoined its members to fight against the laws wherever they appeared.[58]

The Association might have taken an even more aggressive stand on the Equal Rights Amendment during the twenties had it not discontinued its activities as a national organization in mid-1928. The increased dues eliminated so many members that the NAWL stopped publication of its journal and did not hold its annual meeting for two years. Without these two methods of communication, the Association had no way of carrying on any sort of activity. Clearly the existence of a separate women's organization was tenuous at best, and clearly the majority of women attorneys had no interest in it. Perhaps the misfortunes of the late twenties helped to build a stronger organization in the thirties. When the NAWL resumed operation in 1930, its membership was smaller but more dedicated since the luke-warm members had departed. Also, the Association had a clear and aggressive program based on equality for women in the legal profession and support of the Equal Rights Amendment.[59] But the absence of this decisiveness, in addition to their minority status among women lawyers as well as within the profession, prevented the members of the NAWL from achieving their goal of professional equality in the twenties.

Past experience had taught women doctors and lawyers the value of cooperative group effort. The suffrage movement owed its success to organized women as did the passage of the Cable and Sheppard-Towner Acts. Almost invariably, women doctors who were famous during the twenties would probably not have achieved their positions without the help of other females along the way. Most of the physicians trained in women's schools or hospitals, and lay women provided them with financial aid, spiritual support, and clients. The Washington College of Law served the same function for hopeful women attorneys that the Medical College did for future doctors. Consequently, when the expected advances in the professions did not materialize during the twenties, some professional women naturally thought in terms of their own organizations. With many veterans of the suffrage movement in their ranks, women doctors and lawyers had both leadership and expertise at their fingertips.

But the women veterans of the suffrage movement who made their plans to improve their status in the professions did not sufficiently take into account the growth of professionalism among younger women doctors and attorneys. The entire selection and training process of the 1920's helped to develop professional spirit in the young women.

Admissions officers in medical colleges frankly acknowledged that they demanded a higher degree of dedication from prospective female applicants than from male candidates.[60] Certainly the sacrifices entailed in professional training—money, time and personal life—served to discourage those women who did not want a life-long career. Significantly, women physicians and lawyers supported the rising standards for admission to the schools even though the requirements hurt the chances for female applicants.[61] Throughout the training period, students absorbed not only the technical knowledge of their craft but also the ethics and behavior patterns of their profession. Those who could not adapt left the program.[62] Emilie M. Bullowa traced the development of professional spirit in the novice lawyer from an attitude of personal ambition through a stage of pride in being a lawyer, emerging as a selfless love of the law.[63] By the time the young doctor and attorney were ready to start practice, they had become accustomed to thinking in terms of the profession and of themselves as professionals.

Membership in a profession meant accepting the values of the group as one's own. Because the ethics and mores of the learned professions stressed objectivity and emotional detachment, the stridency of the rhetoric of the MWNA and the NAWL grated on the ears of conservative doctors and attorneys.[64] Demands for rights, warned Emilie M. Bullowa, was unprofessional behavior: "Not the seeking of positions, but the fitting ourselves to serve in positions of responsibility and trust—this should be our sacred duty as Women Lawyers of America.[65] Often understated, the message was nevertheless quite clear: women would win an equal place in the professions by the quality of their work, not by aggressive arguments. Desire for approval from their professional peers, who, after all, controlled appointments and honors and were a major source of referrals and recommendations, weighed heavily against the solidarity and elusive promises of the women's organizations. Despite the fact that, as females, they had fought against their traditional roles, the majority of women doctors and lawyers chose not to fight against their conservative professions.

The reasons why women lawyers and doctors decided to form their own societies were understandable. As ignored minorities, they needed support and encouragement. The organizations provided vehicles for combatting discrimination within the professions and for carrying out their own special projects. Yet the time was not auspicious for women's professional groups. Because the twenties experienced a backlash against feminism and radicalism, the programs of the NAWL and the MWNA could be stigmatized by opponents as radical and feminist organizations. The legal and medical professions had just made what appeared to be major concessions to women when they opened the doors of their national associations and admitted more females to their training schools. Many women were content with the lowering of these barriers and were afraid to risk their advances by making more demands and antagonizing the men.   Then too, the whole process of becoming a professional reduced the possibility that women would join either organization.

The MWNA and the NAWL were not useless organizations. They pricked the consciences of the professions and kept alive the determination to secure equality for women in the professions among a small number of their sex.   The medical women provided important humanitarian and educational services as well.   If it were true that the organizations made little headway during the twenties in their major goal of improving the status of women doctors and lawyers, it was equally true that those women who chose the other route of quiet acceptance of their position likewise did little to improve the lot of professional women.

NOTES

[1] Among the other women's professional groups founded during the twenties were the Berkshire Conference of Women Historians, the Association of Women Architects, and the Society of Women Geographers. The women graduate students in the Department of Chemistry at the University of Chicago started a sorority, Kappa Mu Sigma, to encourage other women to pursue careers in chemistry. Most of these organizations were small, but they gave the women the encouragement and support that might not be forthcoming from the regular professional associations dominated by men.

[2] Lopate, *Women in Medicine,* 20.

[3] Gilb, *Hidden Hierarchies,* 48.

[4] Moore, *The Professions,* 158-160.

[5] Morton, *A Woman Surgeon,* 165-167; Fishbein, *History of the American Medical Association,* 263.

[6] Van Hoosen, *Petticoat Surgeon,* 201.

[7] Ibid, 201-202.

[8] Esther Pohl Lovejoy, "American Women's Hospitals," *Medical Review of Reviews* 37 (March, 1931), 149-156; Morton, 269-293.

[9] Significantly, all of the MWNA members also belonged to the AMA, and the women's organization held its meetings in conjunction with the AMA conventions. Van Hoosen, *Petticoat Surgeon,* 202.

[10] "Official Report of the Annual Meeting of the Medical Women's National Association,"*MWJ* 28 (July, 1921), 173; "Report of the Twelfth Convention of the Medical Women's National Association," *MWJ* 33 (May, 1926), 129.

[11] "President Tracy's Address," *MWJ* 27 (May, 1920), 133.

[12] Ibid., 134.

[13] "The Boston Meeting," *MWJ* 28 (June, 1921), 147.

[14] Ibid.

[15] "Equal Rights for Women Doctors," *MWJ* 29 (October, 1922), 261.

[16] See Table 1 in the Appendix.

[17] Florence Brown Sherbon, "Women in Medicine," *MWJ* 33 (September, 1925), 240-241.

[18]Bertha Van Hoosen, "Opportunities for Medical Women as Interns," *MWJ* (March-December, 1926), and 34 (January-May, 1927).

[19]Idem, "Opportunities for Women to Do Research in Medicine," *MWJ* 37 (June, 1930), 162-164; "Opportunities for Medical Women." *MWJ* 34 (June, 1927), 173-175; "Report of the Committee on Medical Opportunities for Women," *MWJ* 35 (July, 1928), 198-199.

[20]"The Modern Pioneer," *MWJ* 37 (April, 1930), 102-103; "Report of the National Committee on Medical Opportunities for Women," *MWJ* 37 (July, 1930), 200-202; Bertha Van Hoosen, "Women Doctors as Members of Medical Societies," *MWJ* 36 (October, 1929), 276.

[21]"Fourteenth Convention of the Medical Women's National Association," *MWJ* 35 (June, 1928), 170.

[22]"Resolutions Adopted by the Annual Convention," *MWJ* 37 (July, 1930), 196-197.

[23]Inez C. Philbrick, "Women, Let Us Be Loyal to Women," *MWJ* 36 (February, 1929), 41.

[24]"President Tracy's Address," 133.

[25]The merger did not materialize, and the New York Infirmary is still in operations today. *MWJ* 33 (April, 1926), 111; "Gotham Hospital," *MWJ* 36 (April, 1929), 87-89.

[26]Lemons, *The Woman Citizen*, 42.

[27]Mabel E. Gardener, "The Danger of Isolation," *MWJ* 31 (October, 1924), 290-291.

[28]Florence Brown Sherbon, "Our Novitiates," *MWJ* 33 (July, 1926), 191-192.

[29]Kate Campbell Mead, "Amalgamation, Not Segregation," *MWJ* 30 (August, 1923), 246.

[30]Sherbon, "Our Novitiates," 192; Philbrick, 41.

[31]"Resolutions Adopted by the Annual Convention," 197.

[32]Clara G. Gottschalk, "Report of the Fifteenth Annual Meeting of the Medical Women's National Association," *MWJ* 36 (August, 1929), 210.

[33]In 1922 and 1927, the Board of Trustees of the AMA tabled resolutions aimed at changing existing laws that prohibited dissemination of information on birth control. Fishbein, 328, 371.

[34]Philbrick, 42; Idem, "Significant Steps and Auguries toward and of State Medicine," *MWJ* 35 (May, 1928), 123-128; Baker, *Fighting for Life*, 239.

[35]Katherine R. Pike, "National Association of Women Lawyers," *WLJ* 18 (April-October, 1930), 14-15.

[36]"National Association of Women Lawyers," *WLJ* 15 (January, 1927), 3.

[37]The *WLJ* printed its membership list in each edition.   In January, 1925, the list contained over four hundred names. Later that year, the Association weeded out those who had not paid their dues, thus shortening the list considerably.   No membership lists appeared after 1925.

[38]Pike, 14.

[39]"National Association of Women Lawyers," 3.

[40]Ibid.

[41]Theresa Doland, "Women Lawyers," *Michigan State Bar Journal* 6 (November, 1926), 46.

[42]"Sane Suggestion," *WLJ* 14 (October, 1926), 9.

[43]"National Association of Women Lawyers," 3.

[44]"Women Members of the ABA," *WLJ* 15 (January, 1927), 3-4.

[45]*WLJ* 10 (July, 1921), 29; See also "Address of Emilies M. Bullowa," *WLJ* 13 (October, 1924), 5.

[46]When a suggestion was made to take an opinion poll on the Blanket Equality Bill in 1922, the treasurer of the Association said that it was impossible to finance the project. "Blanket Equality Bill," *WLJ* 12 (December, 1922-January, 1923), 14.

[47]Ellen Spencer Mussey, "Report of the Committee on Legal Education," *WLJ* 15 (October, 1927), 9.

[48]The *WLJ* tried to establish a Belva Lockwood Scholarship of $1000 for the use of women students of the Washington College of Law in the early twenties.   But no mention of it appeared later in the journal, leading one to assume that the money was never raised.

[49]The trend died out after the early 1920's and women wrote ther own technical articles. Two of those written by men were: Edward J. Dooley, "Necessity of a Family Court," *WLJ* 10 (October, 1920), 1-2; Thomas L. T. Crain, "Religious Instruction for the Young," *WLJ* 10 (January, 1921), 9-10.

[50]Emilie M. Bullowa, "Address," *WLJ* 13 (January, 1924), 5-10.

[51]"Emilie Bullowa's Address," *WLJ* 10 (April, 1921), 18-19.

[52]In 1925, the *WLJ* ran a forum for discussion of the Child Labor Amendment.   The response was heavily negative.

[53]"Blanket Equality Bill," 12, 14.

[54]Ibid., 14.

[55]Ibid., Reba Talbot Swain,"Our Attitude On Legislation," *WLJ* 12 (October-November, 1922), 5.

[56]Rosa Falls Bres, "Shall there Be Special Restrictive Laws for Women?" *WLJ* 15 (July, 1927), 4.

[57]Ibid.; Lemons, 203.

[58]Bres; Marion Gold Lewis, "Proceedings of the Annual Meeting at Buffalo, N. Y., August 29 and 30," *WLJ* 15 (October, 1927), 5.

[59]Lillian D. Rock, "The Need for and the Purpose of the National Association of Women Lawyers," *WLJ* 18 (April-October, 1930), 15-17.

[60]Bertha Van Hoosen, "Quo Vadis?" *MWJ* 36 (January, 1929), 1-4; Idem, "Report of the National Committee on Medical Opportunities for Women," *MWJ* 37 (July, 1930), 200-202.

[61]"Address of Ruth Lewinson," *WLJ* 13 (April, 1924), 13-14; "A Diminished Profession," *MWJ* 27 (September, 1920), 233.

[62]Pavalko, *Sociology of Occupations and Professions*, 82; Howard M. Vollmer and Donald L. Mills, eds., *Professionalization* (Englewood Cliffs, N.J.: Prentice-Hall, 1966), 18.

[63]Lopate, 20; Bertha Rembaugh, "Women in the Law," *New York University Law Review* 1 (April, 1924), 19-20.

[65]Bullowa, "Address," 10.

CHAPTER VI

THE DECADE OF ELUSIVE PROMISE: SUMMARY AND CONCLUSION

Dr. Elizabeth K. Adams remarked in her 1921 book on professional opportunities for women that

> New doors have been set ajar and old doors set wider open. They [women] stand at the beginning of a period which may be notable for their professional as well as their political enfranchisement and progress.[1]

Her statement was not naively optimistic because it was based on fact. Most professional schools had opened their doors to female students, and women had increased their numbers and proportions in those institutions. Despite a withdrawal of women workers from industry following the Armistice, the number of women attorneys and college teachers had continued to rise. Professional associations had finally admitted women to membership on the same basis as men. More important, a few women in medicine, law, and higher education were receiving awards, honors, and appointments in recognition in their contributions to their professions. Despite the knowledge that there was still a long way to go to achieve equality with their male colleagues, professional women were confident that the twenties would be a decade of progress in this struggle.

By the end of the twenties, it was clear that professional women had not realized this expectation. The number of women in medical schools and practice had declined while those in law and higher education had made only modest gains. Furthermore, in all three fields, female practitioners concentrated in the lower ranks or in marginal positions. They were not steadily rising within their callings. What was not clear was why this was happening.

That there were more factors operating against women's entry and success in the professions than there were working for them should be evident. To begin with, the pool from which candidates for medicine, law, and college teaching came was small. Historically, the professions have drawn their members largely from the middle and upper classes which had a tradition of learning and the money and leisure to pursue higher education. Even though expansion of colleges during the twenties offered opportunities to women from all levels of society, the extra cost of advanced training limited professional careers mainly to women of the upper classes. In addition, in many middle-class families, a son, rather than a daughter, was the likely candidate to receive financial assistance for college and professional training. Families expected sons to become bread-winners of their own households and daughters to be supported by their husbands.

Regional variations were noticeable as well. Professional women were more likely to be found in urban, rather than rural areas, particularly in the Northeast, the Midwest and the Pacific states. This pattern may have reflected the availability of training facilities since there were far more medical, law, and graduate schools open to women in those regions than in the South or Great Plains States.[2] Both men and women discovered cities provided more opportunities for employment or practice than small towns offered. In cities, female professionals were not unique, which made it easier for women to break the old patterns. Certainly in the South women had a difficult time following their callings. Betty Reynolds Cobb, an attorney who worked in her husband's law office in Carrollton, Georgia, complained that clients never asked her for legal opinions although they knew she had a law degree. She said, "I would not advise any young woman to study law with a view of practicing it below the 'Mason and Dixon Line' for the next generation at least."[3] The absence of active female professionals in large areas of the country reduced the likelihood of young girls in those regions choosing careers as doctors, lawyers, or college instructors.

Despite the recent improvements for women in the professions, there was still little to encourage women to pursue careers during the twenties. The social norms of the day still epitomized woman's primary role as wife and mother. Although many women worked, it was assumed that their jobs were temporary, something to be relinquished when the women married. By definition, professions were life-long careers, and therefore woman's entry into those occupations was contrary to society's expectations. In addition, many men and women strongly suspected that women had neither the ability nor the character to handle professional careers. Clients were reluctant to seek out women practitioners, and within the professions, sexual prejudice was a fact of life. Some men actively discriminated against female practitioners, but others simply ignored women. The results were virtually the same in either case; women were tolerated rather than welcomed by their male colleagues. For women to succeed in the professions, it took not only marked ability but also determination to withstand the pressures and prejudices of society.

One other factor that may have affected women professionals was the general employment situation for females. The twenties was a decade of economic boom, even despite an early post-war recession and another slight recession in 1927. But women did not appear to share equally in the prosperity. Even before the later recession, women found it increasingly difficult to find positions that suited their qualifications and abilities. From 1925 onward, different Bureaus of Placement for trained women around the country reported that employers seemed reluctant to hire new applicants or to give them good salaries. Directors of the Bureaus assumed that certain segments of the economy were stagnating and that businesses were no longer willing to experiment with women in responsible positions.[4] While most women doctors and some attorneys were self-employed, those in salaried positions may have felt the economic pinch. The employment situation may also have influenced some families trying to decide whether or not to finance a professional education for their daughters.

Taken together, such factors as class and regional distribution, the expectations of society, sexual prejudice, and the employment situation weighed heavily against women's entry or success in the learned professions. While the lowering of institutional barriers was a definite plus in favor of women, it did not eliminate these continuing problems.

Nor did the recent advances compensate for the changes occurring within the professions themselves. Medicine, law, higher education, and many other occupations as well, were attempting to deal with their own crises.[5] Leaders in these fields were concerned about keeping up with the expansion of knowledge in their areas and with the demands of the public for more and better services. Complaints from within the professions about declining income and prestige in the face of the rising business community vied for attention with worries about the intrusions of non-professionals into the work domain of certified practitioners. The leaders of these callings responded to the problems by attempting to professionalize their occupations. They improved and lengthened training programs, tightened admissions through stricter certification rules and examinations, and gained greater control over practitioners through the use of their professional organizations.

Professionalization produced mixed results. The higher standards for admission to professional schools and the longer duration of their programs increased the cost in time and money of joining these occupations. In addition, school officials used the new requirements to select the best qualified applicants and, sometimes, to keep out "undesirables." Stricter licensing laws acted as an additional sieve. The end products were better educated professionals and, in some fields, fewer practitioners. Service to the community improved because there were fewer incompetents and charlatans than there had been earlier, but the public paid more for those services. Another consequence of professionalization was that many women as well as members of the lower classes and minority groups found professional training beyond their reach. The majority of practitioners were, consequently, white, middle-class males.

Although the pattern of professionalization was similar for all three fields, conditions in each affected women's possibilities for success. Of the three professions, medicine was the most difficult and expensive to enter. By the twenties, the profession was ten years into its reform program, and the AMA had substantially reduced the number of medical schools, students, and practitioners. Because the future reward of status and income were, on the average, greater than for the other fields, competition to get into medical school rose sharply. The shortage of physicians placed a premium on training people who would be likely to practice for many years; and because it was assumed, though not substantiated, that a high percentage of women would drop out of medicine to marry and raise families, school officials were extremely careful in screening female applicants. In consequence, the few women who managed to win admission to the profession were capable and dedicated. Yet because of discrimination in internships, residencies, and hospital privileges, women found themselves in marginal specialties, less remunerative practices, and subordinate positions on staffs of institutions and businesses. As a tiny minority, women doctors had no voice in the power-structure of the profession.

Women lawyers had many opportunities for training during the twenties largely because of the inability of the legal profession to stem the growth of part-time schools. The existence of such institutions, however, may have been a mixed blessing for women. Because the ABA was trying to improve the profession, employers looked closely at the training of prospective legal clerks and partners. Women who took part-time courses had enough legal training to make efficient secretaries or clerical workers but not enough to become law partners. A very small proportion of women attorneys studied at approved institutions in the twenties. Women faced the additional problem linked to their recent enfranchisement and late start in the profession: strong prejudices from male lawyers and clients of both sexes hindered women's advancement. Women attorneys had not, as yet, carved out a "female specialty," and they had little to offer prospective employers other than their ability to do the tedious background work for low salaries.

Education was the easiest of the three fields for women to enter and the one offering the greatest possibilities for advancement. A combination of fortuitous events helped to explain the situation. Higher education, particularly for women, expanded tremendously during the twenties and created a demand for college teachers. because the salaries in academia were relatively low, men may not have been attracted to the profession as much as to other callings, thus giving women an extra advantage. Then too, women found there was less of a stigma attached to females in college teaching than in medicine or law. Women had a traditional place in the profession, and they dealt with fresh-faced youths in a relatively sheltered environment, rather than with hardened criminals or the ravages of diseases. Furthermore, the existence of strong, independent women's colleges provided some women with the chance to rise within their own fields and within the academic hierarchy. Despite these favorable conditions, few women in academics managed to achieve the heights of the profession in the twenties. The majority ended up in "female subjects," in small schools, and in the lower ranks of the profession.

Although individual factors affected women's progress in each field, certain common patterns emerged. There was a cumulative effect: a woman's training influenced the kind of position she obtained; this in turn influenced how far she would climb. Whether it was because of lack of motivation, discouragement, financial problems, or discrimination, women had a difficult time securing the best available training. Harvard was the top law school, but it did not accept women; medical women found it far easier to obtain residencies in pediatrics than in surgery; and in academics, many women did not pursue Ph.D.s because the rewards were not commensurate with the costs. As a consequence, women in all three callings went into "female fields." Women doctors treated women and children and the poor or held salaried positions; female attorneys did the research which their male coworkers used in presenting court cases; and academic women taught languages and humanities in small colleges rather than doing research in universities. In each case, the fields in which women concentrated were outside the paths, established and monitored by the male hierarchy, that led to preferment, honors, and power.

Women were handicapped in another way. Dr. Adams noted that the professions in the early twenties were showing a new concern about placing novice members.[6] Sheer numbers and the rapid changes in standards made it impossible for any one individual to have first-hand knowledge of all candidates or of all positions. As a result, placement and advancement occurred frequently through informal channels, many of which were closed to women. Paper credentials were supplemented by personal recommendations through the "old boy" system. Recommending a protege meant the patron's investing a part of his own prestige in the performance of the student. In the case of women, unknown quantities in the eyes of many male professionals, there was always the lurking fear that they would not live up to expectations or would marry and leave the profession.[7] Thus women often had difficulty securing strong recommendations that would help them begin their careers.

The question naturally arises as to why women did not actively try to improve their status within the professions. After all, they fought so many traditions and prejudices to become doctors, lawyers, or college teachers, it seemed logical that women would refuse to accept a lowly status in their occupations. In part, this may have resulted because women were selected for certain characteristics but not for others. The medical profession demanded a high degree of dedication from female applicants, and such women may not have found the time or inclination to emerge in battles which would take too much time away from patients. In a sense, dedication was its own reward.

Some women did protest against the status quo in their occupations. Small groups of medical and legal women, largely excluded from the power structure of the AMA and ABA, formed their own professional organizations for support and to have a vehicle for improving their positions within the professions. These women discovered, however, that their associations had some negative results. The organizations emphasized the separateness and the minority status of women within the professions, while their programs and political views often branded the associations as militant or radical. The demands of these women for equal treatment were usually interpreted as requests for special privileges or seen as an unwillingness among women to shoulder their share of the burden. The majority of women doctors and lawyers, fully aware of their minority position within their profession and desirous of acceptance by their male colleagues, eschewed association with these organizations. They were content with recent, if limited, gains made by their sex and were unwilling to antagonize the male members of the professions by making more demands. Feminine solidarity did not compare with belonging to the profession in the eyes of most women lawyers and physicians.

A fuller explanation of women's inaction would include the process of socialization through which all professionals went. While training to be doctors, lawyers, or educators, the students learned the ethics and etiquette of their calling. They learned to be good professionals as well as good practitioners, and as a result, they emerged with a sense that they had a personal stake in the well-being of their profession. Socialization helped to perpetuate the status quo in these conservative occupations. The process may have affected women more than men. As a suspect minority group already outside the norms proscribed by society, women were constantly under pressure to prove their professionalism. They were careful about giving vent to emotional outburst and protests against blatant discrimination because such behavior was considered "unprofessional." It appears that almost all women professionals, whether they belonged to the women's professional organizations or not, agreed that the best way for women to win acceptance from the male establishment was to excel at their calling.

The drive for professionalization was a pervasive influence during the twenties. Many occupations increased their requirements for admission to training schools, lobbied for certification laws, and formed associations to monitor the practitioners. Although the vocational literature warned girls planning careers to obtain the best education and training available because of the rising standards, it is questionable if many women realized what was happening in the world of occupations.[8] Nor was it clear what the long-term impact of professionalization would be.

The effects of professionalization—the policies and patterns established or solidified during the twenties—continued to influence the professions until the late 1960's. Admissions standards for training and certification rose rather than fell, and the paths to appointment and advancement remained substantially unchanged. The socialization process continued to turn out loyal professionals. As a consequence, the proportion of women in medicine and law inched up slowly while in college teaching it declined. Women practitioners continued to be invisible members in their callings, relegated to subordinate, unimportant positions.

Only since the late sixties has there been a reversal in the trend of professionalization. In the wake of the civil rights movement, professional schools have lost their absolute control over admissions policies, and publicly supported institutions are likewise under pressure to conform with state and federal guidelines in regard to hiring and advancement practices. Younger professionals have shown a reluctance to accept without question the status quo in their occupations. By the same token, the revival of feminism has reawakened interest among women in professional careers. Not only have opportunities for women in professional schools increased, but also their enrollment in those institutions has grown markedly in the past six years. A few women are receiving superior positions and appointments, which is encouraging to young girls planning their futures. Significantly, women are more interested in fighting the status quo in the professions, and they have formed a number of associations to carry out this goal.[9]

Of course, it is too soom to tell whether the recent changes represent a lasting trend toward greater participation of women in the professions or if the seventies will prove to be another decade of elusive promise. No one can accurately predict the impact of the economy, social mores, and political events on women's participation in these occupations. In the twenties, career women read the signs of the time and predicted that the decade would witness great strides forward in the quest for equal status with men in the professions. Women professionals had no way of calculating the impact of professionalization on their opportunities for entrance and advancement within their chosen fields. The removal of institutional obstacles was neutralized by changes that professional women had not foreseen, and the hoped-for progress predicted in the early years of the decade had not materialized.

NOTES

[1] Adams, *Women Professional Workers*, 18.

[2] "Biennial Survey of Education, 1928-1930."

[3] Betty Reynolds Cobb to Emma P. Hirth, April 9, 1920, BVI Papers, Box 11, Law: Letters from Women Lawyers.

[4] "Annual Report of the Managing Director of the Chicago Collegiate Bureau of Occupations, 1925-1926," WEIU Papers, Box 10, Folder AB; "Statistical Reports of the Philadelphia Bureau of Occupations for 1926-1927," WEIU Papers, Box 16, Folder AB.

[5] Among the other occupations that were raising their standards for admission were: dentistry, engineering, ministry, music, social work, library work, and nursing. See appropriate sections of BVI, *Training for the Professions and Allied Occupations*, and Fleischman, *An Outline of Careers for Women*.

[6] Adams, 394-395.

[7] Pavlako, *Sociology of Occupations and Professions*, 162-164.

[8] Adams; Fleischman; BVI, *Training for the Professions and Allied Occupations*; Hatcher, *Occupations for Women*.

[9] For the most recent developments see the following: "Medical Education in the United States, 1973-1974," *JAMA* 231 (January, 1975),supplement; Rudolph C. Blitz, "Women in the Professions, 1870-1970," *Monthly Labor Review* 97 (May, 1974), 34-35; John B. Parrish, "Women in Professional Training," *Monthly Labor Review* 97 (May, 1974), 41-43; Millard H. Rudd, "That Burgeoning Law School Enrollment is Portia," *ABAJ* 60 (February, 1974), 182-184; Shirley Raissi Bysiewicz, "1972 AALS Questionnaire on Women in Legal Education," *Journal of Legal Education* 25 (1973), 503-513.

APPENDIX

TABLE 1

Annual Enrollments in U. S. Medical Schools,
By Sex, Each Year, 1904-1930

Year	Students Enrolled*			Females as Percentage of Total Enrollment
	Both Sexes	Males	Females	
1904	28,142	27,013	1,129	4.8
1910	21,526	20,619	907	4.5
1911	19,786	19,106	680	3.4
1912	18,412	17,733	679	3.7
1913	17,015	16,373	640	3.8
1914	16,502	15,871	631	3.8
1915	14,891	14,299	592	4.0
1916	14,012	13,446	566	4.0
1917	13,764	13,154	610	4.5
1918	13,630	13,049	581	4.3
1919	12,930	12,244	686	5.3
1920	13,798	12,980	818	5.9
1921	14,466	13,587	879	6.0
1922	15,635	14,646	989	6.3
1923	16,960	15,930	1,030	6.0
1924	17,728	16,774	954	5.4
1925	18,200	17,290	910	5.0
1926	18,840	17,905	935	4.9
1927	19,662	18,698	964	4.9
1928	20,545	19,616	929	4.5
1929	20,878	19,953	925	4.4
1930	21,597	20,642	955	4.4

SOURCE: "Medical Education Numbers" for 1910-1930 in the *Journal of the American Medical ociation.*
*The enrollment figures are for the academic year ending June 30 of the year listed.

TABLE 2

Annual Graduates of U. S. Medical Schools, By Sex, Each Year, 1904-1930

Year	Graduates*			Females as Percentage of Total Graduates
	Both Sexes	Males	Females	
1904	5,574	5,376	198	3.5
1910	4,440	4,324	116	2.6
1911	4,273	4,114	159	3.7
1912	4,483	4,341	142	3.2
1913	3,981	3,827	154	3.8
1914	3,594	3,473	121	3.4
1915	3,536	3,444	92	2.6
1916	3,518	3,384	134	3.8
1917	3,379	3,226	153	4.5
1918	2,670	2,564	106	4.0
1919	2,656	2,549	107	4.0
1920	3,047	2,925	122	4.0
1921	3,192	3,041	151	4.7
1922	2,529	2,375	154	6.1
1923	3,120	2,906	214	6.9
1924	3,562	3,348	214	6.0
1925	3,974	3,770	204	5.1
1926	3,962	3,750	212	5.4
1927	4,035	3,846	189	4.7
1928	4,262	4,055	207	4.9
1929	4,446	4,232	214	4.8
1930	4,565	4,361	204	4.5

SOURCE: "Medical Education Numbers" for 1910-1930 in the *Journal of the American Medical Association.*

*The graduation figures are for the academic year ending June 30 of the year listed.

TABLE 3

Biennial Enrollment in U. S. Law Schools,
By Sex, Each Year, 1920-1930

Biennial Enrollment in All U. S. Law Schools,
By Sex, Each Year, 1920-1930

Year	Students Enrolled			Females as Percentage
	Both Sexes	Males	Females	of Total Enrollment
1920	20,969	19,803	1,166	5.6
1922	28,920	27,275	1,645	5.7
1924	35,830	33,763	2,067	5.8
1926	40,643	38,454	2,189	5.4
1928	41,858	39,677	2,181	5.2
1930	39,213	37,010	2,203	5.6

Biennial Enrollment in Approved* Law Schools,
By Sex, Each Year, 1920-1930

Year	Students Enrolled			Females as Percentage
	Both Sexes	Males	Females	of Total Enrollment
1920	10,926	10,545	381	3.5
1922	12,103	11,540	563	4.7
1924	13,845	13,299	546	3.9
1926	14,773	14,333	440	2.9
1928	15,235	14,811	424	2.8
1930	16,307	15,784	523	3.2

Biennial Enrollment in Approved Law Schools as
Percentage of Enrollment in All Law Schools,
By Sex, Each Year, 1920-1930

Year	Both Sexes	Males	Females
1920	52.1	53.2	32.7
1922	41.2	42.3	34.2
1924	38.6	39.4	26.4
1926	36.3	37.3	20.1
1928	36.4	37.3	19.4
1930	41.6	42.6	23.7

SOURCE: U. S., Bureau of Education, "Biennial Survey of Education," 1920-1930.
*Approved law schools were those belonging to the Association of American Law Schools fore 1922 and those approved by the American Bar Association after 1922.

TABLE 4

Biennial Graduates of U. S. Law Schools, By Sex, Each Year, 1920-1930

Biennial Graduates of All U. S. Law Schools, By Sex, Each Year, 1920-1930

Year	Graduates			Females as Percentage of Total Graduates
	Both Sexes	Males	Females	
1920	3,342	3,165	177	5.3
1922	5,216	4,967	249	4.8
1924	6,833	6,435	398	5.8
1926	8,117	7,685	432	5.3
1928	8,648	8,204	444	5.1
1930	8,714	8,303	411	4.7

Biennial Graduates of Approved* Law Schools, By Sex, Each Year, 1920-1930

Year	Graduates			Females as Percentage of Total Graduates
	Both Sexes	Males	Females	
1920	1,678	1,641	37	2.2
1922	2,352	2,290	62	2.6
1924	2,893	2,781	112	3.9
1926	3,104	3,016	88	2.8
1928	3,490	3,399	91	2.6
1930	3,539	3,449	90	2.5

Biennial Graduates of Approved* Law Schools as Percentage of Graduates of All Law Schools, By Sex, Each Year, 1920-1930

Year	Both Sexes	Males	Females
1920	50.2	51.8	20.9
1922	45.1	46.1	24.9
1924	42.3	43.2	28.1
1926	38.2	39.2	20.4
1928	40.4	41.4	20.5
1930	40.6	41.5	21.9

SOURCE: U. S., Bureau of Education, "Biennial Survey of Education," 1920-1930.
*Approved law schools were those belonging to the Association of American Law Schools before 1922 and those approved by the American Bar Association after 1922.

TABLE 5

Biennial Enrollment and Advanced Degrees in U. S.
Graduate Schools, by Sex, Each Year, 1918-1930

Biennial Enrollment in U. S. Graduate Schools,
by Sex, Each Year, 1918-1930

Year	Students Enrolled			Females as Percentage of Total Enrollment
	Both Sexes	Males	Females	
1918	14,406	8,497	5,909	41.0
1920	15,612	9,837	5,775	36.3
1922	23,016	15,046	7,970	34.6
1924	28,799	18,444	10,355	35.9
1926	32,500	20,159	12,341	37.9
1928	44,165	26,540	17,625	39.9
1930	47,255	29,070	18,185	38.8

Biennial Advanced Degrees in U. S. Graduate
Schools, by Sex, Each Year, 1918-1930

Year	Graduates			Females as Percentage of Total Graduates
	Both Sexes	Males	Females	
1918	3,480	2,320	1,160	33.3
1920	4,853	3,457	1,396	28.8
1922	7,327	5,445	1,882	25.6
1924	9,261	6,447	2,814	30.3
1926	11,451	7,700	3,751	32.7
1928	13,834	8,976	4,858	35.1
1930	16,832	10,693	6,139	36.6

SOURCE: U. S., Bureau of Education, "Biennial Survey of Education," 1918-1930.

TABLE 6

Annual Ph.D. Recipients of U. S. Graduate Schools, By Sex, Each Year, 1920-1930

Year	Ph.D. Recipients			Females as Percentage of Total Ph.D. Recipients
	Both Sexes	Males	Females	
1920	560	470	90	16.0
1921	660	553	107	16.2
1922	780	667	113	14.5
1923	1,062	905	157	14.7
1924	1,124	957	167	14.8
1925	1,203	1,000	203	16.8
1926	1,438	1,241	197	13.7
1927	1,538	1,308	230	14.9
1928	1,617	1,385	232	14.3
1929	1,907	1,587	320	16.7
1930	2,058	1,747	311	15.1

SOURCE: Lindsey R. Harmon and Herbert Soldz, *Doctoral Production in United States Universities, 1920-1962* (Washington, D. C.: National Academy of Science and National Research Council, 1963).

BIBLIOGRAPHY

I. MAJOR TOOLS

The following is a list of the most helpful references for learning about the professions in the 1920's and women's position within them.

American Law School Review.
Contains lists of law schools approved by the Association of American Law Schools, regulations for admission to the bar for all states, and, after 1922, enrollment figures for all law schools. The statistics do not account for drop-outs or mid-year matriculants, and they are broken down according to class year but not according to sex.

American Medical Association. *Index Medicus.*
An international guide to medical literature. Headings under "Education, Medical" and "Medical Profession" are helpful, but there are few entries under "Physicians, Women."

Astin, Helen. *Women: A Bibliography on Their Education and Careers.* Washington, D.C.: Human Service Press, 1971.
Though primarily for recent years, there is a section on historical works.

Breckinridge, Sophonsiba P. *Women in the Twentieth Century: A Study of Their Political, Social and Economic Activities.* New York: McGraw-Hill Book Company, Inc., 1933.
One of the monographs resulting from the survey made by the President's Research Committee on Social Trends. It covers the progress of women from 1900 to 1930 and is filled with statistics and insights. Perhaps the best starting place for finding out about women's activities outside the home for this period.

James, Edwart T.; James, Janet Wilson; and Boyer, Paul S. *Notable American Women, 1607-1950: A Biographical Dictionary.* 3 vols. Cambridge, Mass.: Belknap Press, 1971. Well-written short biographies with references.

Journal of the American Medical Association.
Particularly useful for an official view on most topics of interest to the profession. In April or May of each year it carries "State Board Statistics" for the preceding year which gives the number of applicants for licensure, their institutions, and their success or failure. In August or September, the AMA publishes its "Medical Education in the United States," which gives statistics for enrollment and graduates of all medical schools in the United States and Canada by sex and by race. The series also includes requirements for all schools, internship and residency programs, and requirements for certification. Of the three professions, medicine appears to have had the most accurate statistics for the 1920's.

The Law Student.
From 1923-1930, it contained incomplete lists of states administering bar exams and their results. It was the only single source for this kind of information.

President's Research Committee on Social Trends. *Recent Social Trends in the United States.* New York: McGraw-Hill Company, Inc., 1933.
Compilation of the monographs on various aspects of American society. Good insights and references.

Theodore, Athena, compiler. *The Professional Women.* Cambridge, Mass.:   Schenkman Publishing Company, 1971.
Predominantly sociological or psychological articles on women in the professions and their problems.   Helpful for theory and footnotes.

U. S., Department of the Interior, Bureau of Education.   "Bulletins of the Bureau of Education, 1906-1927."   *Bulletin,* No. 17 (1928).
An index of the bulletins published for those years.

_____.   "Biennial Survey of Education: Statistics of Universities, Colleges, and Professional Schools."   *Bulletin.*
Contains enrollment, graduation, and faculty statistics by sex for each institution of higher education listed.   Also includes financial statements, degrees awarded, and programs offered.   The Bureau relied on voluntary reporting and gave no guidelines for defining "student," "enrollment period," or "faculty."   Statistics are incomplete and suggestive at best but still the best available for the period.   It is the only source for the 1920's to tabulate law school enrollments by sex.

Vollmer, Howard M. and Mills, Donald L., eds. *Professionalization.* Englewood Cliffs, N.J.:   Prentice-Hall, 1966.
Useful collection of articles on the topic with references.

Wilson, H. L.   *Index to Legal Periodicals.*
International guide to articles in legal journals.   Heading of "Legal Profession" and "Legal Education" are helpful.   Few entries appear under "Women Lawyers."

Women Studies Abstracts.
Current articles on all aspects of women's studies including history.

II. PRIMARY SOURCES

Manuscripts

Arthur and Elizabeth Schlesinger Library on the History of Women in America, Radcliffe College, Cambridge, Massachusetts.

American Association of University Women Papers.
Primarily concerned with the activities and programs of the association rather than with professional women.

Bureau of Vocational Information Papers.
A veritable gold mine.   An extensive collection (thirty-eight boxes) based on letters, questionnaires, interviews, and clippings used to assemble the various studies of the BVI.

Particularly useful for information on women in law, chemistry, personnel work, and statistical work. One of the few collections dealing with the problems of career women during the twenties.

Institute of Women's Professional Relations Papers.
An interesting collection from an organization that tried to continue and expand on the work done by the BVI after its demise in 1926.

Morgan-Howe Papers.
Includes papers of Ethel Puffer Howe, main force behind the Institute for the Coordination of Women's Interests at Smith College during the twenties. The Institute was an experiment to try and combine the roles of career and homemaker for women.

Somerville-Howorth Family Papers.
Contains the paper of Lucy Somerville Howorth, a prominent lawyer and clubwoman during the twenties. Rather disappointing on women in the legal profession.

Women's Educational and Industrial Union Papers.
Papers of the first occupational bureau specializing in vocational information for college alumnae. Particularly useful for the historical background on the vocational guidance movement.

Government Documents and Publications

U. S., Department of Commerce, Bureau of the Census. *Fifteenth Census of the United States, 1930: Population.* Vol. 4, *Occupations by United States, 1930: Population.* Vol. 4, *Occupations by States.*

U. S., Department of Commerce, Bureau of the Census. *Fifteenth Census of the United States, 1930: Population.* Vol. 5, *General Report on Occupations.*

_____. *Fourteenth Census of the United States, 1920: Population.* Vol. 4, *Occupations.*

_____. *Historical Statistics of the United States, Colonial Times to 1957.* Washington, D.C.: Government Printing Office, 1960.

_____. *Thirteenth Census of the United States, 1910: Population.* Vol. 4, *Occupation Statistics.*

_____. *Women in Gainful Employment, 1870 to 1920: A Study of the Trends of Recent Changes in Number, Occupational Distribution, and Family Relationships of Women Reported in the Census as Distribution, and Family Relationships of Women Reported in the Census as Following a Gainful Employment,* by Joseph A. Hill. Census Monograph 9 (Washington, D.C.: Goverment Printing Office, 1929).
Helpful, but difficult to use in conjunction with census statistics because they used different cut-off points for ages.

U. S., Department of the Interior, Bureau of Education. "Legal Education, 1925-1928." *Bulletin*, No. 31 (1929).
Brief Summary of progress and needs of legal education.

_____. "Medical Education, 1918-1920." *Bulletin*, No. 15 (1921).
Appearing biennially, a brief report on the progress and needs of medical education. Not a substitute for the annual reports on medical education appearing in *JAMA*.

_____. "Recent Progress in Legal Education." *Bulletin*, No. 3 (1926).

_____. *Opportunities for the Study of Medicine in the United States*, by George Frederick Zook. Washington, D.C.: Government Printing Office, 1920.
A publication meant to attract foreign students with a brief history of the recent progress in the reform of medical education.

_____. "Self-Help for College Students." *Bulletin*, No. 2 (1929).
A remarkable document. Advice on how to work one's way through college and statistics on students who did just that. Also contains a list of all accredited institutions of higher education, their affiliation, and their tuition and fees for 1927-1928.

U. S., Department of the Interior, Bureau of Education. "Scholarships and Fellowships: Grants Available in United States Colleges and Universities." *Bulletin*, No. 15 (1929).
List of scholarships available and awarded in 1927-1928. Breakdown according to sex, year in school, discipline, institution, and requirements.

U. S., Department of Labor, Women's Bureau. *Annual Reports*. 1920-1930.
Illustrate the struggle that the Women's Bureau had to stay alive in the face of small annual budgets.

_____. "The New Position of Women in American Industry." *Women's Bureau Bulletin*, No. 12 (1920).
Women's contribution during the war.

_____. "Occupational Progress of Women: An Interpretation of Census Statistics of Women in Gainful Occupations." *Women's Bureau Bulletin*, No. 27 (1922).

_____. "The Occupational Progress of Women, 1910-1930." *Women's Bureau Bulletin*, No. 104 (1933).

_____. "Women in Government Service." *Women's Bureau Bulletin*, No. 8 (1920).
The report that caused the Civil Service Commission to open all exams to both sexes.

Books

Adams, Elizabeth Kemper. *Women Professional Workers: A Study Made for the Women's Educational and Industrial Union.* New York: Macmillan Company, 1921.
A perceptive study of professions and other careers for trained women. Dr. Adams seemed aware of the changes occurring in occupations in the early twenties. Particularly helpful for its history on the development of vocational guidance.

Allen, Frederick Lewis. *Only Yesterday: An Informal History of the Nineteen-Twenties.* New York: Harper and Brothers, 1931.
One of the influential volumes contributing to the myth of women's economic emancipation in the 1920's.

Arnett, Trevor. *Teachers' Salaries in Certain Endowed and State Supported Colleges and Universities in the United States, with Special Reference to Colleges of Arts, Literature and Science, 1926-1927.* Publication of the General Education Board. *Occasional Papers*, No. 8 (1928).
Useful compilation of data.

Baker, Sara Josephine. *Fighting for Life.* New York: Macmillan Company, 1939.
Delightfully written autobiography of the founder of the first bureau of child hygiene in the world. Particularly interesting for information of women in the public health movement and politics in New York City.

Blackford, Katherine M. H. and Newcomb, Arthur. *The Right Job: How To Choose, Prepare for, and Succeed in It.* Garden City, N. Y.: Doubleday, Page and Company, 1925.
Matching a person to the right job by analyzing his or her physical traits. Not much help to my study.

Booth, Meyrick. *Women and Society.* New York: Longmans, Green and Company, 1929.
One of the traditionalists who believed that biology was destiny and that working women were a menace to society.

Bureau of Vocational Information. *Training for the Professions and Allied Occupations: Facilities Available for Women in the United States.* New York: Bureau of Vocational Information, 1924.
The most comprehensive compilation of training opportunities for women available in the 1920's. Contains assessments of women's opportunities in various fields and information on tuition, fees, scholarships, loan programs, and requirements for certification.

Collier, V. M. *Marriage and Careers: A Study of 100 Women Who Are Wives, Mothers, Homemakers and Professional Workers.* New York: Bureau of Vocational Information, 1926.
An attempt to show that it was possible to combine marriage and careers successfully.

Doerschuk, Beatrice. *Women in the Law: An Analysis of Training, Practice and Salaried Positions.* New York: Bureau of Vocational Information, 1920.
The best single published source on women lawyers for the 1920's. Based on questionnaires, letters, and reports from women lawyers and law schools. Gives prospects for women, their salaries, and kind of education and training to get.

Dublin, Louis I. *Health and Wealth.* New York: Haper and Brothers, 1928.
Series of lectures focusing on the problems of population. Dublin thought continued growth of population was beneficial to the nation and consequently did not approve of women, who should have been raising families, working outside the home.

Elliott, Margaret and Manson, Grace. *Earnings of Women in Business and the Professions.* Ann Arbor: Universiity of Michigan School of Business, Bureau of Business Research, 1930.
Based on a survey made of members of the National Federation of Business and Professional Women's Clubs in the late 1920's. Useful information and statistics.

Fleischman, Doris E., ed. *An Outline of Careers for Women: A Practical Guide to Achievement.* Garden City, N. Y.: Doubleday, Doran and Company, 1928.
Series of articles by top women in many fields. Not as good as the BVI studies but still useful. A clear-eyed picture of what it took to reach the top in a career.

Flexner, Abraham. *Medical Education in the United States and Canada: A Report to the Carnegie Foundation for the Advancement of Teaching.* New York: Carnegie Foundation· for the Advancement of Teaching, 1910.
Besides being a major impetus in the reform of medical education, this volume is also one of the best compilations of information and statistics on the history of medical education in the United States up to 1910.

Good, Carter V. *Teaching in College and University: A Survey of Problems and Literature of Higher Education.* Baltimore: Warwick and York, 1929.
An extensive bibliography but little on the development of the academic profession.

Hamilton, Alice. *Exploring the Dangerous Trades.* Boston: Little Brown, 1948.
Interesting autobiography of a pioneer in industrial medicine and an ardent reformer. Disappointing on her years at Harvard, where she was the first female member of the faculty.

Hatcher, Orie Latham. *Occupations for Women: Being the Practical Information Obtained by a Study Made for the Southern Woman's Educational Alliance.* Richmond, Va.: Southern Woman's Educational Alliance, 1927.
Good information on job opportunities for women in the South. Does not gloss over the difficulties of finding and keeping a good position.

Henderson, Yandell and Davie, Maurice R. *Incomes and Living Costs of a University Faculty.* New Haven, Conn.: Yale University Press, 1928-29.
Yale University Professors could not live on their salaries. Good statistics.

Leuck Miriam Simons. *Fields of Work for Women.* New York: D. Appelton and Company, 1926.
Aimed at young women with high school degrees. Practical advice, but of little use to my study.

Manson, Grace E. *Occupational Interests and Personality Requirements of Women in Business and the Professions.* Ann Arbor: University of Michigan School of Business, Bureau of Business Research, 1931.
Based on a survey made of the members of the National Federation of Business and Professional Women's Clubs. Useful information and statistics.

Morton, Rosalie Slaughter. *A Woman Surgeon*. New York: Frederick A. Stokes, 1937.
Interesting autobiography on an early leader of the MWNA and the force behind the
American Women's Hospitals. A little early for the status of women doctors in the
1920's.

Ogg, Frederic Austin. *Research in the Humanistic and Social Sciences*. New York: The
Century Company, 1928.
Useful reference for research institutes, projects, and sources of financial aid in the
twenties.

Peixotto, Jessica B. *Getting and Spending at the Professional Standard of Living*. New
York: Macmillan Company, 1927.
A solid study of members of a university faculty and the difficulty they had living on
their academic salaries.

Pruette, Loraine. *Women and Leisure: A Study of Social Waste*. New York: Dutton
and Company, 1924.
Examines the dynamics of wasted female talent. The major deterrents are unrealistic
goals of young women, lack of guidance, and prejudice.

Reed, Alfred Zantzinger. *Training for the Public Profession of the Law: Historical
Development and Principal Contemporary Problems of Legal Education in the United
States with Some Accounts of Conditions in England and Canada*. New York: D. B.
Updike, 1921.
The major survey of legal training and its history in the United States.   Excellent
information and statistics.

_____. *Present-Day Law Schools in the United States and Canada*. New York: D.
B. Updike, 1928.
Updates information in his 1921 volume, showing the progress of reform in legal
education.   Excellent statistics for the twenties.

Ross, Edward Alsworth. *The Social Trend*. New York: The Century Company, 1922.
A noted sociologist of the day speaking of several aspects of social changes, including
women.   He sees women as mothers of the race.

Slosson, Preston William. *The Great Crusade and After, 1914-1929*. New York:
Macmillan Company, 1930.
A good survey of the twenties by a contemporary author. He thought the decade was
one of emancipation for women.

Thwing, Charles Franklin. *A History of Higher Education in America*. New York: D.
Appelton and Company, 1906.
Primarily useful for his views on the teaching profession.

Van Hoosen, Bertha. *Petticoat Surgeon*. Chicago: Pelligrini and Cudahy, 1947.
Autobiography of the founder of the MWNA who was also a prominent obstetrician,
surgeon, and medical teacher in her day. Somewhat confusing and annoying because of
what she leaves out (dates, etc.).

Withington, Alfreda Bosworth. *Mine Eyes Have Seen: A Woman Doctor's Saga.* New York: E. P. Dutton, 1941.
Autobiography of a woman physician who spent the 1920's in the Tennessee hill country treating the residents.

Zook, George F. and Haggerty, M. E. *The Evaluation of Higher Institutions,* Vol. 1: *Principles of Accrediting Higher Institutions.* Chicago: University of Chicago Press, 1936.
Brief history of the development of accrediting agencies.

Major Periodicals

American Magazine, 1919-1930, all issues.
A wide-circulation family magazine. Valuable because it shows what the average American was likely to think and read about the career woman.

Annals of the American Academy of Political and Social Sciences 143 (May, 1929).
Entitled "Women in the Modern World," this issue contains perceptive, well-documented articles on various aspects of women. Clear-eyed assessment of where women stood at the end of the twenties.

Bulletin of the American Association of University Professors. 1916-1930, all issues.
Covers controversies and problems of the academic profession. Lists new members and their institutions and contains complete reports of the committees of the organization.

Carnegie Foundation for the Advancement of Teaching. *Annual Reports.* 1915-1930, all issues.
Summaries of the progress of the various programs of the foundations, including the results of the surveys on the medical, dental, and legal professions and their attempts to reform professional education.

Independent Woman. 1920-1930, all issues.
The official journal of the National Federation of Business and Professional Women's Clubs, this is a must for anyone working on career women in the 1920's. It gives insights into the social, political, and economic views of the organization and of career women.

Journal of the American Association of University Women. 1920-1930, all issues.
Contains some well-written and researched articles on women in the professions.

Medical Woman's Journal. 1919-1931, all issues.
Official journal of the Medical Women's National Association, it is the best published source on women doctors and their activities in the twenties. Thanks to Dr. Van Hoosen's surveys, there is solid information on women in internships, salaried positions, medical schools, and medical societies. Contains information on the political views and activities of the association as well as technical articles on medicine.

Proceeding of the Association of American Universities. 1900-1930, all issues.
Compilation of the papers and discussions of the annual meetings of the association.

Actually rather disappointing because it has relatively little about the academic profession. Concentrates heavily on graduate education.

Woman Citizen (Woman's Journal after 1928). 1919-1931, all issues.
Formerly the official journal of the National American Women's Suffrage Association, it is a must for anyone studying women in the 1920's. It contained articles, letters, and comments on women's activities outside the home, including: politics, jobs, the arts, and volunteer work.

Women Lawyers Journal. 1920-1930, all issues.
The journal of the National Association of Women Lawyers, it is much smaller than its medical counterpart. Despite irregular publication (no issues in the summer and none between mid-1928 and 1930) and inadequate articles, this is still about the only published source that voiced the opinions of women lawyers on major political and professional issues during the twenties.

Selected Articles

Aley, Robert J. "Education for the Law." *Law Students' Helper* 20 (February, 1912), 49.

Angell, James R. "Economic Conditions and Educational Opportunities for Students to Obtain a Legal Education Requiring Two Years of College Training." *American Bar Association Journal* 144 (March, 1922), 144-145.

Archer, Gleason L. "Facts and Implications of College Monopoly of Legal Education." *American Law School Review* 6 (January, 1930), 576-584.
Dean of a part-time law school criticizing the AALS.

"Are Many Women Replacing Soldiers in Industrial Work?" *Current Opinion* 64 (January, 1918), 60-61.

Arnett, Trevor. "Teachers' Salaries." *Association of American Colleges Bulletin* 5 (March, 1929), 9-19.
Faculty salaries had risen substantially; they were more than keeping pace with the cost of living.

Armstrong, Anne W. "Are Business Women Getting a Square Deal?" *Atlantic Monthly* 140 (July, 1927), 28-36.

Babcock, Kendrice C., Ph.D. "Needed Revisions in Medical Licensure in Accordance with Present-Day Medical Education." *Journal of the American Medical Association* 80 (April 28, 1923), 1262-1264.

"Banking Milestone." *Bankers' Magazine* 106 (June, 1923), 1106-1107.

Barker, F. D. "Determining the Fitness of Premedical Students." *Bulletin of the Association of American Medical Colleges* 2 (January, 1927), 16-21.

Bass, Elizabeth. "Scholarship Loan Fund of the Medical Women's National Association." *Medical Review of Reviews* 37 (March, 1931), 162-164.

Bates, Henry M. "Should Applicants for Admission to the Bar Be Required to Take a Law School Course?" *Case and Comment* 21 (May, 1925), 960-961.

Bierwirth, J. C. "The Medical Profession: The Necessity and Benefits from its More Complete Organization." *Journal of the American Medical Association* 35 (August 11, 1900), 335-337.

Bolton, Frederick E. "College Teaching as a Career for Men." *School and Society* 21 (February 21, 1925), 213-217.

Bunzel, Bessie. "Woman Goes to College, after Which, Must She Choose Between Marriage and a Career?" *Century Magazine* 117 (November, 1928), 26-33.

Byrne, Joseph. "Problem of an Ailing Medical Profession and Its Solution." *Medical Record* 98 (September 25, 1920), 514-519.

Cabot, Richard C. "Women in Medicine." *Journal of the American Medical Association* 65 (September 11, 1915), 947-948.
He thought they really belonged in only a few fields such as pediatrics.

Carson, Hampton L. "An Existing Defect in the American System of Legal Education." *American Law Review* 48 (November-December, 1914), 859-873.

Clark, Charles E. "The Law School and the Student: Admission and Exclusion of Students." *American Law School Review* 7 (April, 1932), 397-400.
About the policy of restricting class size adopted by some schools in the late twenties.

Charters, W. W. "Graduate Schools and College Teaching." *Educational Research Bulletin* 7 (November 14, 1928), 348-349.
Discusses the need for graduate schools to have courses on teaching techniques.

Cohen, Jules Henry. "Lay Practices of the Law Injures Client, Not Legal Profession." *Journal of the American Judicature Society* 5 (August, 1921), 52-53.
About the infringement by notaries public, corporations, and trust companies on the legal profession and what to do about it.

"College Education as a Pre-Requisite to the Practice of Law." *Virginia Law Register* n.s. 8 (May, 1922), 51-52.

Colwell, N. P. "Can the Poor Boy Secure a Medical Education?" *Journal of the American Medical Association* 81 (August 18, 1923), 577-578.

_____. "Present Needs of Medical Education." *Journal of the American Medical Association* 82 (March 15, 1924), 838-840.

"Commercialism in Medicine." *Journal of the American Medical Association* 38 (April 5, 1920), 879-880.

Cook, Walter W. "Improvement of Legal Education and Standards for Admission to the Bar." *American Law School Review* 4 (1917), 338-345.

_____. "Council on Legal Education: A Plan for the Improvement of Legal Education and Standards for Admission to the Bar." *American Law School Review* 4 (1917), 241-254.

Cottle, Marion Weston. "The Prejudice Against Women Lawyers: How Can It Be Overcome?" *Case and Comment* 21 (October, 1914), 371-373.

Craig, Hardin. "Method of Appointment and Promotion in American Colleges and Universities." *Bulletin of the American Association of University Professors* 15 (March, 1929), 175-217.
Faulty technique but interesting and useful statistics.

Curtis, A. C. "Woman as a Student of Medicine." *Bulletin of the Association of American Medical Colleges* 2 (April, 1927), 140-148.
Survey made of students at the University of Michigan Medical School. Women were equal to if not better than men.

Curtis, Winterton C. "Recruiting of the College and University Profession." *School and Society* 11 (January 3, 1920), 14-18.
Disappointing article. Muddled argument.

Davison, Wilburt C. "Selection of Medical Students." *Southern Medical Journal* 20 (December, 1927), 955-960.

Doland, Theresa. "Women Lawyers." *Michigan State Bar Journal* 6 (November, 1926), 44-47.

"Faculty Training in the Liberal Arts College: A Report of the Committee on Faculty Scholarship." *North Central Association Quarterly* 3 (September, 1928), 172-179.
Very good information and statistics on faculty attainment of advanced degrees.

"Fellowships and Scholarships." *Journal of the Association of American Medical Colleges* 4 (April, 1929), 1-36.

Flexner, Abraham. "Medical Colleges." *World's Work* 21 (April, 1911), 75-91.

_____. "Medical Education." *Educational Record* 5 (April, 1924), 75-91.

Ferson, Merton L. "Law Aptitude Examinations." *American Law School Review* 5 (December , 1925), 563-565.

"Fetish of the Job." *Harper's Magazine* 151 (November, 1925), 731-738.

Gile, John M. "Medical Education and Medical Supply." *Boston Medical and Surgical Journal* 185 (September 29, 1921), 387-390.

Giles, Isabel. "The Twentieth Century Portia." *Case and Comment* 21 (October, 1914), 353-357.

Goodsell, Willystine. "Educational Opportunities of American Women—Theoretical and Actual." *Annals of the American Academy of Political and Social Sciences* 143 (May, 1929), 1-13.

Haggerty, Melvin E. "Occupational Destination of Ph.D. Recipients." *Educational Record* 9 (October, 1928), 209-218.
Discusses the failure of graduate schools to produce productive researchers.

Hale, William G. "Legal Education and Admission to the Bar." *Oregon Law Review* 1 (April, 1921), 1-9.

Harper, Ellahue Ansile. "How to Raise the Standard of Morals for the Legal Profession." *Dickinson Law Review* 93 (January, 1925), 93-102.

Hartt, Rollin Lynde. "Woman Physician: Has She Arrived After Her Long and Adventurous Struggle?" *Century Magazine* 114 (July, 1927), 337-345.
Short history of women in medicine. Not particularly good.

Herrick, W. W. "Trend in Modern Medical Education." *Southern Medical Journal* 13 (May, 1920), 381-387.

"Higher Educational Standards Urged for Admission to Study Law in New York." *American Law School Review* 6 (May, 1927), 137-145.

Hitchcock, Nevada Davis. "Mobilization of Women." *American Academy of Political and Social Sciences* 78 (July, 1918), 24-31.
About the Women's Committee of the CND and its organization of women's volunteer activities during World War I.

Hitchler, Harrison. "College Graduation as an Entrance Requirement to Law Schools." *Law Notes* 18 (January, 1915), 188-192.

Hopkins, Grace. "Women's Work in the Courts in the United States." *Journal of Comparative Legislation* n.s. 15 (1915), 198-202.

Horack, H. C. "Supply and Demand in the Legal Profession." *American Bar Association Journal* 14 (November, 1928), 567-572.

"Hospitals Approved for Internships." *Journal of the American Medical Association* 88 (March 12, 1927), 818-825.

Hughes, Agnes Lockhart. "Meet the Lady Bankers, Gentlemen!" *Outlook* 127 (March 23, 1921), 462-463.

Hurlin, Ralph G. "Educational Research and Statistics." *School and Society* 12 (October 30, 1920), 412-414.
About the need to raise teachers' salaries.

Hutchinson, Emilie J. "Women and the Ph.D." *Journal of the American Association of University Women* 22 (October, 1928), 19-22.
An excellent study with revealing statistics on women with doctoral degrees.

Jernegan, Marcus W. "Productivity of Doctors of Philosophy in History." *American Historical Review* 33 (October, 1927), 1-22.

"Labor Shortage." *New Republic* 12 (October 20, 1917), 316-317.

Leigh, Robert D. "College Teaching as a Career." *Journal of the National Education Association* 18 (January, 1929), 9-10.
Negative view of the profession.

Lillie, C. W. "What Shall We Do To Be Saved—Professionally?" *Illinois Medical Journal* 42 (July, 1922), 28-31.

Lonn, Ella. "Academic Status of Women on University Faculties." *Journal of the American Association of University Women* 17 (January-March, 1924), 5-11.
A fine study that added to the information on women in the academic profession. Helpful statistics.

Lovejoy, Arthur O. "Annual Message of the President." *Bulletin of the American Association of University Professors* 5 (November-December, 1919), 10-40.

Lovejoy, Esther Pohl. "The American Women's Hospitals." *Medical Review of Reviews* 37 (March, 1931), 149-156.

Ludovici, Anthony M. "Woman's Encroachment on Man's Domain." *Current History* 27 (October, 1927), 21-25.

Lynch, Thomas R. "Too Many Lawyers?" *American Law Review* 61 (January 22, 1927), 914-917.

"Making the Law a Learned Profession." *Central Law Journal* 93 (September 23, 1921), 201-203.

Martin, Paul L. "Shall the Standard Law Course Be Extended to Four Years?" *Illinois Law Review* 11 (December, 1916), 351-359.

May, Elizabeth P. "Occupations of Wellesley Graduates." *School and Society* 29 (February 2, 1929), 147-148.
Shows the declining proportion of women going into teaching careers.

"Medical Education in the United States: Editorial." *Journal of the American Medical Association* 93 (August 17, 1929), 547-548.

"Medical Education for Women." *Journal of the American Medical Association* 38 (May 17, 1902), 306-307.

"Medical Education for Women." *Journal of the American Medical Association* 38 (May 31, 1902), 1451.

"Medical Organization." *Journal of the American Medical Association* 37 (July 6, 1901), 30-31.

"Menace of a Plutocratic Bar." *Journal of the American Judicature Society* 5 (February, 1922), 131-132.

"More Diploma Mills." *Journal of the American Medical Association* 81 (November 3, 1923), 1541-1544.

Mosher, Eliza M. "Woman Doctor Who Stuck it Out." *Literary Digest* 85 (April 4, 1925), 66-69.

Mussey, Ellen Spencer. "Women Attorneys." *American Bar Association Journal* 9 (January, 1923), 62-63.

Myers, Burton D. "Disposition of Applicants for Admission to Schools for 1926-1927." *Bulletin of the Association of American Medical Colleges* 2 (April, 1927), 97-104. This and similar articles provide fine statistics showing the rising populartity of medicine as a career and the growing competition to get into medical school.

_____. "Report on Applications of Matriculation in Schools of Medicine for 1927-1928." *Bulletin of the Association of American Medical Colleges* 3 (July, 1928), 193-199.

_____. "Report on Applications for Matriculation in Schools of Medicine in the United States and Canada, 1928-1929." *Journal of the Association of American Medical Colleges* 4 (April, 1929), 97-110.

_____. "Report on Applications for Matriculation in Schools of Medicine of the United States and Canada, 1920-1930." *Journal of the Association of American Medical Colleges* 5 (March, 1930), 65-87.

Nicolson, Marjorie. "Scholars and Ladies." *Yale Review* n.s. 19 (June, 1930), 775-795.

Norris, Jean H. "The Women Lawyers' Association." *Case and Comment* 21 (October, 1914), 364-366.

Olney, Richard. "To Uphold the Honor of the Profession of Law." *Yale Law Journal,* 19 (March, 1910), 341-344.

Painter, Charles F. "Educational Requirement for Twentieth Century Practice." *Boston Medical and Surgical Journal* 194 (June 10, 1926), 1057-1065.

Palmer, Clara F. "Women in Medicine." *Journal of the Oklahoma Medical Association* 13 (September, 1920), 340-341.
Primarily about the relief work women doctors did during and after World War I and their lack of recognition.

Pearl, Raymond. "Distribution of Physicians in the United States: Commentary on the Report of the General Education Board." *Journal of the American Medical Association* 84 (April 4, 1925), 1024-1028.

Pettus, Isabella Mary. "Legal Education of Women." *Albany Law Journal* 61 (May 26, 1900), 325-331.
General history of women lawyers and evaluation of their work in 1900.

Phillips, R. LeClerc. "The Problem of the Educated Woman." *Harper's Magazine* 154 (December, 1926), 57-63.
Written by a woman, it discusses the harm supposedly caused by spinster teachers in women's colleges.

Pinkham, Charles B. "Study in Diplomas." *Journal of the American Medical Association* 83 (July 26, 1924), 290-294.
About sale of fraudulent medical diplomas.

Pound, Roscoe. "The Law School and Professional Tradition." *Michigan Law Review* 24 (December, 1925), 156-165.

"Preliminary Report of Committee W on the Status of Women in College and Universiity Faculties." *Bulletin of the American Association of University Professors* 7 (October, 1921), 21-32.
An excellent source for finding out about the status of women in the academic profession and the attitudes of male colleagues toward women.   Good statistics.

"The Question of Women's Colleges." *Atlantic Monthly* 140 (November, 1927), 577-584.
Plea for more financial support for women's schools.

Reed, Alfred Z. "The Lawyer as a Privileged Servant of Democracy." *Journal of the American Judicature Society* 6 (February, 1923), 154-156.

_____. "Raising Standards of Legal Education." *American Bar Association Journal* 7 (November, 1921), 571-578.

_____. "Rising Bar Admission Requirements and Evening Law Students." *American Bar Association Journal* 15 (July, 1929), 429-431.

Rembaugh, Bertha. "Women in the Law." *New York University Law Review* 1 (April, 1924), 19-23.

Rich, Stephen G. "College Teaching as a Career." *School and Society* 22 (October 17, 1922), 495-496.

Robinson, Lelia J. "Women Lawyers in the United States, with Portraits." *Green Bag* 2 (January, 1890), 10-32.

Rude, Anna E. "The Sheppard-Towner Bill in Relation to Public Health." *Journal of the American Medical Association* 79 (September 16, 1922), 959-964.

Sanderson, Suzanne. "Women Physicians." *Journal of the Michigan Medical Society* 30 (May, 1931), 339-344.

"Second Report of Committee W on the Status of Women in College and University Faculties." *Bulletin of the American Association of University Professors* 10 (November, 1924), 65-73.
Excellent source for statistics on academic women and the attitudes toward female teachers.

"Shall Women Lose Their New Jobs?" *Literary Digest* 60 (January 11, 1919), 14-15.
About women's position in the post-war labor force.

Shuler, Marjorie. "Organization of Business Women." *Review of Reviews* 66 (September, 1922), 309-310.
About the National Federation of Business and Professional Women's Clubs.

"Status of Women in College and University Faculties." *School and Society* 21 (January 3, 1925), 16-17.
About the survey made by Committee W of the AAUP.

Stone, Harlan F. "The Future of Legal Education." *American Law School Review* 5 (May, 1924), 329-344.

_____. "Legal Education and Democratic Principle." *American Bar Association Journal* 7 (December, 1921), 639-646.

Thayer, Ezra R. "Law Schools and Bar Examinations." *American Law School Review* 3 (November, 1913), 374-381.

Tracy, Martha. "The Profession of Medicine and Women's Opportunities in This Field." *Journal of the American Association of University Women* 21 (October, 1927), 5-10.
Good article stressing Dr. Tracy's belief that there no longer existed barriers to women becoming doctors.

_____. "Women Graduates in Medicine." *Bulletin of the Association of American Medical Colleges* 2 (January, 1927), 21-28.
Useful article showing that women did not drop out of medical practice. Some statistics that are helpful.

_____. "Women in Medicine." *Bulletin of the Association of American Medical Colleges* 3 (October, 1928), 327-328.
Updates her earlier article in the *Bulletin.*

_____. "Women's Medical College of Pennsylvania." *Medical Review of Reviews* 37 (May, 1931), 157-161.
Brief history of the institution.

Vance, W. R. "Is the Legal Profession Losing its Influence in the Community?" *Central Law Journal* 91 (July 30, 1920), 77-78.

Van Rensselaer, Mrs. Coffin. "The National League for Woman's Service." *Annals of the American Academy of Political and Social Science* 79 (September, 1918), 275-282.

"Vocational Information for Women." *School Review* 29 (October, 1921), 565-566. About the Bureau of Vocational Information and its services.

Ward, George Gray, Jr. "Relation of Medical Profession to the Community." *Medical Record* 99 (February 26, 1921), 337-339.

Watters, Ethel M. "Child Hygiene and the Sheppard-Towner Fund." *Southern Medical Journal* 17 (March, 1924), 189-195.

Weiskotten, H. G. "Study of Present Tendencies in Medical Practice." *Bulletin of the Association of American Medical Colleges* 3 (April, 1928), 130-144. Good article with statistics showing the trend toward specialization.

Welpton, Martha. "Women Physicians." *Journal of the Michigan Medical Society* 50 (May, 1931), 341-342.

Wembridge, Eleanor Rowland. "Professional Education of Women and the Family Problem." *Social Hygiene* 6 (April, 1920), 181-196.

Wickser, Philip J. "Bar Associations." *Cornell Law Quarterly* 15 (April, 1930), 390-419. Brief history and statistics on bar associations. Plea for greater organization within the legal profession.

Wilbur, Ray Lyman. "Saving Time in Medical School." *Journal of the American Medical Association* 86 (May 15, 1926), 1498.

Wolfe, A. B. and Olsen, H. "War-Time Industrial Employment of Women in the United States." *Journal of Political Economy* 27 (October, 1919), 639-669. Perceptive article with helpful statistics.

"Woman's Work after the War." *New Republic* 17 (January 25, 1919), 358-359. Primarily about women in industry.

"Women and the Labor Shortage." *Scientific American* 119 (September 14, 1918), 206.

"Women as Lawyers: Mrs Goodell's Case." *Central Law Journal* 3 (March 24, 1876), 186.

"Women at the Bar." *Law Notes* 27 (October, 1923), 124.

"Women in Medicine." *Saturday Evening Post* 200 (January 21, 1928), 22.

Wormser, I. Maurice. "Fewer Lawyers and Better Ones." *American Bar Association Journal* 15 (April, 1929), 206-210.

_____. "Problem of the Evening Law Schools." *American Law School Review* 4 (November, 1920), 544-547.

Zapffe, F. C. "Analysis of Entrance Credentials Presented by Freshman Admitted in 1929." *Journal of the Association of American Medical Colleges* 5 (July, 1930), 231-234.

III. SECONDARY SOURCES

Books

American Bar Foundation. *Compilation of Published Statistics on Law School Enrollments and Admissions to the Bar, 1889-1957.* N.P.: American Bar Foundation, 1957.
Statistics for enrollment taken from the *American Law School Review* annual compilations. This is a convenient tool.

Berelson, Bernard. *Graduate Education in the United States.* New York: McGraw-Hill, 1960.
Brief, text-book treatment of the subject. Good references. This is an area that needs more investigation.

Bernard, Jessie. *Academic Woman.* University Park, Pa.: Pennsylvania State University Press, 1964.
Although primarily about women college teachers in the 1950's and 1960's, it provides some history and many insights into the problems of women in the professions.

Bluemel, Elinor. *Florence Sabin: Colorado Woman of the Century.* Bolder, Col.: University of Colorado Press, 1959.
Based on the personal papers of Dr. Sabin, this book tends to degenerate into annecdotes in parts. It does not provide a clear picture of the struggles women had in the medical profession.

Brown, Esther Lucille. *Physicians and Medical Care.* New York: Russell Sage Foundation, 1937.
A little late for my study but it does have some useful statistics.

Brubacher, John S. and Rudy, Willis. *Higher Education in Transition: A History of American Colleges and Universities, 1636-1968.* Revised and enlarged. New York: Harper and Row, Publisher, 1968.
A good general survey in a text-book approach. Useful bibliography.

Carr-Saunders, A. M. and Wilson, P. A. *The Professions.* Oxford: Clarendon Press, 1933.
The classic study on the history and development of the professions. Although it is about the British professions, it provides marvelous insights that are applicable to conditions in the United States.

Chafe, William H. *The American Woman: Her Changing Social, Economic, and Political Roles, 1920-1970.* New York: Oxford University Press, 1972.
A path-breaking study. To date, the best single survey of women in the United States in the post-suffrage era. Generally good information despite some notable omissions,

such as the impact of birth control. He raises may interesting questions that will lead to further studies. Useful bibliography and notes.

Clark, Harold Florian. *Life Earnings in Selected Occupations in the United States*. New York: Harper and Brothers, 1937.
A useful study with statistics, notes, and appendices showing median salaries for a wide range of occupations during the twenties and the early thirties. It shows the effect of the Depression.

Council of State Governments. *Occupational Licensing Legislation in the States*. Chicago: Council of State Governments, 1952.
Brief summary of the history, purposes, and pitfalls of licensing legislation for occupations. Contains a chart showing when various occupations obtained the right to licensing in all states. Very helpful, but could use updating.

Earnest, Ernest. *Academic Procession: An Informal History of the American College, 1636-1953*. Indianapolis: Bobbs-Merril, 1953.
Enjoyable reading by an author who believes that college should prepare a person for his lifework.

Fishbein, Morris. *A History of the American Medical Association, 1847 to 1947*. Philadelphia: W. B. Saunders Company, 1947.
Primarily a description of the major questions discussed at the annual AMA conventions. Rather poor history, its main value is in highlighting what the AMA thought was important. Significantly, there is more in this volume on the Women's Auxilliary to the AMA (made up of wives of doctors) than on women physicians.

Flexner, Eleanor. *Century of Struggle: The Woman's Rights Movement in the United States*. Cambridge, Mass.: Belknap Press, 1968.
Still the best single study on the history of the movement from the early 1800's to 1920. Helpful footnotes.

Gilb, Corinne Lathrop. *Hidden Hierarchies: The Professions and Government*. New York: Harper and Row, 1966.
A fine study of the relationship between the professional associations and the government. Some history, and good bibliographical notes.

Gildersleeve, Genevieve N. *Women in Banking: A History of the National Association of Bank Women*. Washington, D.C.: Public Affairs Press, 1959.
Primarily of interest because it discusses how and why a women's professional organization got started.

Griswold, Erwin N. *Law and Lawyers in the United States: The Common Law under Stress*. Cambridge: Harvard University Press, 1964.
A series of lectures delivered to a British audience made up of lawyers. The first three provide a brief history of the legal profession and training for it in the United States.

Gruberg, Martin. *Women in American Politics: An Assessment and Sourcebook*. Oshkosh, Wis.: Academia Press, 1968.

Some useful historical and statistical information, but in view of the recent revival of feminism, this book needs revision.

Harmon, Lindsey R. and Soldz, Herbert. *Doctoral Production in United States Universities, 1920-1962.* Washington, D.C.: National Academy of Science and National Research Council, 1963.
The most reliable statistics on earned Ph.D.s from accredited programs in the United States. It is strictly a statistical work and shows the breakdown of degrees according to sex, discipline, institution, and mean time between B.A. and Ph.D. degrees. Very useful.

Harno, Albert J. *Legal Education in the United States.* San Francisco: Bancroft-Whitney Company, 1953.
Good general survey, particularly helpful on the role of the ABA in education.

Hofstadter, Richard and Hardy, C. Dewitt. *The Development and Scope of Higher Education in the United States.* New York: Columbia University Press, 1952.
A general history on the topic.

Kett, Joseph F. *Formation of the American Medical Profession: The Role of Institutions, 1780-1860.* New Haven, Conn.: Yale University Press, 1968.
Delightfully written and well researched book on the early history of the medical profession. Helpful notes.

Lemons, J. Stanley. *The Woman Citizen: Social Feminism in the 1920's.* Urbana: University of Illinois Press, 1973.
A particular good study on women in public affairs in the 1920's showing that Progressivism did not die in that decade. Excellent notes and bibliographical essay.

Leuchtenburg, Williiam E. *The Perils of Prosperity, 1914-1932.* Chicago: University of Chicago Press, 1958.
Well-written narrative history of the twenties. Good for background, but has little on the professions.

Lopate, Carol. *Women in Medicine.* Baltimore: Johns Hopkins Press, 1968.
Primarily about the difficulties women faced getting into medicine in the 1960's but some history and good insights. Has statistics and useful notes.

Lynn, Kenneth S., ed. *The Professions in America.* Boston: Houghton-Mifflin Company, 1965.
Disappointing because it is too general. Not much information on the development of the professions. It concentrates on the current condition of the professions.

McGlothlin, William Joseph. *The Professional Schools.* New York: Center for Applied Research in Education, 1964.
Adequate brief introduction of how professions developed and the role of professional schools. Predominantly concerned with the current problems of professional schools.

Marks, Geoffrey and Beatty, William K. *Women in White.* New York: Charles Schribner's Sons, 1972.
About women doctors and nurses. Of limited scope and some misinformation. Avoid this book.

Oppenheimer, Valerie K. *The Female Labor Force in the United States: Demographic and Economic Factors Governing its Growth and Changing Composition.* Berkeley: Institute of International Studies, University of California, 1970.
A major economics study which is particularly useful for the period after 1940.

Moore Wilbert Ellis. *The Professions: Roles and Rules.* New York: Russell Sage Foundation, 1970.
Excellent book providing a good introduction to the subject from a sociological point of view. Good bibliogaphy.

Newcomer, Mabel. *A Century of Higher Education for American Women.* New York: Harper and Brothers, Publishers, 1959.
Adequate brief history of the subject.

O'Neill, William L. *Everyone Was Brave: A History of American Feminism.* Chicago: Quadrangle Books, 1969.
Mistitled, this study covers what the author considered to be the failure of feminism. He thinks the only hope for the women in the twenties was the Socialist Party. A controversial and thought-provoking work. Limited notes.

Pavalko, Ronald M. *Sociology of Occupations and Professions.* Itasca, Ill.: F. E. Peacock, 1971.
This is a text-book that provides good basic information on the subject.

Pound, Roscoe. *The Lawyer from Antiquity to Modern Times.* St. Paul: West, 1953.
A general history of the profession which, because of the extensive time-span, is rather brief for the 1920's.

Rothstein, William G. *American Physicians in the Nineteenth Century: from Sect to Science.* Baltimore: Johns Hopkins Press, 1972.
A good, but dry, history of the profession in the 1800's which shows a strong influence of sociological theory. Stresses economic factors and class interests in the development of the profession. Excellent notes and reference material.

Rudolph, Frederick. *The American College and University: A History.* New York: Alfred A Knopf, 1962.
An excellent, well-documented study. One of the best in the field.

Schein, Edgar H. *Professional Education: Some New Directions.* New York: McGraw Hill, 1972.
Contains a helpful definition and description of professions. Primarily concerned with recent problems confronting the professions rather than their history.

Schlaback, Theron F. *Pensions for Professors.* Madison: State Historical Society of Wisconsin, 1963.

A well-documented history of the founding and early years of the Carnegie Foundation for the Advancement of Teaching. Examines its goals and effects on higher education.

Scudder, Vida Dutton. *On Journey.* New York: E. P. Dutton, 1937. Autobiography of a professor at Wellesley College. Contains relatively little about women's position in the academic profession.

Shryock, Richard Harrison. *Medical Licensing in America, 1650-1965.* Baltimore: Johns Hopkins University Press, 1967. An extremely useful, brief study of the subject and of the development of the medical profession. Good notes.

_____. *Medicine and Society in America, 1660-1860.* New York: New York University and Society in America, 1660-1860. *New York: New York University Press, 1960.* Series of lectures on various aspects of medical history. Well-written and informative.

Shryock, Richard Harrison. *Medicine in America: Historical Essays.* Baltimore: Johns Hopkins University Press, 1966. Informative essays on various aspects of medical history, including one on women physicians in the nineteenth century.

Smuts, Robert W. *Women and Work in America,* with a new introduction by Eli Ginzberg. New York: Schocken Press, 1971. One of the few books to assess accurately women's position in the labor force. The author did not think women achieved economic emancipation in the 1920's. Some notes.

Travell, Janet. *Office Hours: Day and Night.* New York: World Publishing Company, 1968. Autobiography of the women who was later physician to President Kennedy. She was a medical student in the 1920's and one of those individuals who did everything successfully and claims to have suffered no handicaps in the profession because of her sex.

Veysey, Laurence R. *The Emergence of the American University.* Chicago: University of Chicago Press, 1965. An excellent if somewhat philosophical study. Well-documented and thought-provoking.

Warren, Charles. *A History of the American Bar.* Boston: Little Brown and Company, 1911. Howard Fertig, Inc. edition, 1966. Not too helpful. Too many quotes, too many cases, and too little analysis.

Woody, Thomas. *A History of Women's Education in the United States.* 2 Vols. New York: The Science Press, 1929. A mammouth study covering all levels of women's education. It is particularly good on the nineteenth century.

Articles

Auersbach, Jerold S. "Enmity and Amity: Law Teachers and Practitioners, 1900-1922." *Perspectives in American History* 5 (1971), 551-601.
A beautifully written and well-documented study of the conflicts in the legal profession in the early twentieth century. Good narrative and analytical history.

Barber, Bernard. "Some Problem in the Sociology of the Professions." *Daedalus* 92 (Fall, 1963), 669-688.
Rather general treatment of the subject and limited mainly to the current problems in the field.

Chapman, Carleton B. "*The Flexner Report* by Abraham Flexner." *Daedalus* 103 (Winter, 1974), 105-117.
Good brief article on the impact of the report on medical education and its goals and courses rather than its impact on the medical profession.

Cogan, Morris L. "Toward a Definition of Profession." *Harvard Educational Review* 23 (Winter, 1953), 33-50.
An adequate general discussion of the various definitions and descriptions then in use. Helpful bibliography.

Cowley, William H. "College and University Teaching, 1858-1958." *Educational Record* 39 (October, 1958), 311-326.
This article seems to be mistitled since it concentrates more on the history of the development of colleges than on college teaching.

Freedman, Estelle B. "The New Woman: Changing Views of Women in the 1920s." *Journal of American History* 61 (September, 1974), 372-393.
An excellent bibliographical survey on the various interpretations of women in the twenties pointing to the need for further research.

Goode, W. J. "Community within a Community: The Professions." *American Sociological Review* 22 (April, 1957), 194-200.
Good theoretical article about the relationship between the professions and the larger community.

————. "Encroachment, Charlatanism, and the Emerging Profession: Psychology, Sociology, and Medicine." *American Sociological Review* 25 (December, 1960), 902-914.
Primarily about sociology as an emerging profession but contains a useful definition and set of characteristics of professions.

Hughes, Everett C. "Professions in Society." *Canadian Journal of Economics* 26 (February, 1960), 54-61.
Contains some thoughts on discrimination in the professions and the role of the professions in society.

Lowther, Florence DeL. and Downes, Helen R. "Women in Medicine." *Journal of the American Medical Association* 129 (October 13, 1945), 512-514.
Shows that women physicians did not drop out of the medical professions. Also gives statistics on their concentration in various specialties and their participation as teachers of medicine in the 1940's.

May, Henry F. "Shifting Perspectives on the 1920's." *Mississippi Valley Historical Review* 43 (December, 1956), 405-427.
A helpful bibliographical survey of the twenties. It says little about women in the decade.

Noggle, Burl. "The Twenties: Historiographical Frontier." *Journal of American History* 53 (September, 1966), 299-314.
A solid bibliographical article which updates May's. Although it says little about women or the professions, it contains many references and suggests areas for further research.

Parsons, Talcott. "Professions and Social Structure." *Social Forces* 17 (May, 1939), 457-467.
This article is frequently cited in the bibliographies of works on the topic of the professions, but it is very difficult to follow.

Rogers, James Grafton. "The Standardization Movement in American Law Schools." *Education Record* 13 (July, 1932), 219-227.
This is a good article on the impact of professionalization on the legal occupation.

Rosner, David Karl and Markowitz, Gerald E. "Doctors in Crisis: A Study of the Use of Medical Education Reform to Establish Modern Professional Elitism in Medicine." *American Quarterly* 25 (March, 1973), 83-107.
An excellent article with extensive documentation on the impact of the Flexner Report and of the reform movement on the medical profession.

Rueschmeyer, Dietrich. "Doctors and Lawyers: A Comment on the Theory of the Professions." *Canadian Review of Sociology and Anthropology* 1 (February, 1964), 17-30.
An interesting article comparing the two occupations in terms of the theory of professionalization.

Sorkin, Alan L. "On the Occupational Status of Women, 1870-1970." *American Journal of Economics and Sociology* 32 (July, 1973).
Examines briefly the broad occupational categories (industry, the professions, etc.) and women's changing representation in them.

Stevens, Robert. "Two Cheers for 1870: The American Law School." *Perspectives in American History* 5 (1971), 405-548.
An excellent, well-documented article on the history and development of legal education. A good follow-up of Alfred Z. Reed's work in the twenties.

Touhey, John C. "Effects of Additional Women Professionals on Ratings of Occupational Prestige and Desirability." *Journal of Personality and Social Psychology* 29 (January, 1974), 86-89.
Apparently, the addition of many women to a profession lowers its prestige in the eyes of society.

Wilensky, H. L. "The Professionalization of Everyone?" *American Journal of Sociology* 70 (September, 1964), 137-158.
Discusses the trend of occupations adopting the trappings of the professions in order to achieve the status and autonomy possessed by such occupations as medicine and law.

INDEX